Sharlot Herself

Selected writings of Sharlot Hall

Edited by
NANCY KIRKPATRICK WRIGHT

with an introduction by
MARGARET F. MAXWELL

Illustrations by Carlos Parra

SHARLOT HALL MUSEUM PRESS
Prescott, Arizona

415 West Gurley Street, Prescott, Arizona 86301

Printed in the United States of America

ISBN 0-927579-04-9

For Fulton

Contents

Illustrations ix

Preface xi

Biographical Introduction—by Margaret F. Maxwell xv

CHAPTER ONE
Child Life Among the Moquis 1

CHAPTER TWO
Log Book of a Mountain Schooner 7

CHAPTER THREE
Roadrunner 27

CHAPTER FOUR
The Trip to Roosevelt 33

CHAPTER FIVE
Alone: The Essential Sharlot 41

CHAPTER SIX
Spring in the Desert 47

CHAPTER SEVEN
The Unmarried Woman 55

CHAPTER EIGHT
Lonesome Valley: Sharlot's Southwest 59

CHAPTER NINE
How Splendid Is Our Past: The Mansion 65

CHAPTER TEN
Called to the Mat 73

CHAPTER ELEVEN
A Bit of Picturesque Western Profanity 81

CHAPTER TWELVE
Wind Song: Sharlot through the Eyes of Friends 87

Acknowledgments 93

Notes 95

Index 103

Illustrations

Sharlot Hall, c. 1920 .... *x*
Sharlot Hall, age 16 .... *xiii*
Sharlot, 1905 .... *xviii*
Hopi Village, c. 1890 .... *3*
Hopi children at play, c. 1900 .... *5*
George Hance Trail, c. 1910 .... *10*
Hance Cabin at the Grand Canyon, 1900 .... *23*
Construction workers at Roosevelt Dam site, 1905 .... *34*
Mail wagon on Fish Creek Hill, 1905 .... *39*
Sharlot at Orchard Ranch, c. 1900s *42*
Alice Hewins and Sharlot at the ranch, c. 1924 .... *45*
Sharlot Hall c. 1918 .... *46*
Sharlot in desert c. 1910 .... *49*
Sharlot warily approaches cactus, c. 1910 .... *51*
The Hall family, 1905 .... *57*
Orchard Ranch in winter, c. 1890 .... *60*
Working on the tack at Orchard Ranch, c. 1900 .... *63*
The Governor's Mansion as Sharlot first saw it, c. 1880s *67*
Governor's Mansion during Sharlot's curatorship, c. 1940 .... *71*
Sharlot poses in the copper sheath dress, c. 1925 .... *77*
Sharlot and Alice Hewins, c. 1910 .... *90*
Sharlot and the Reverend Charles Franklin Parker, c. 1940 .... *92*
Sharlot and unidentified friends flying over Los Angeles in a staged studio photograph, c.1910 .... *Back Cover*

All photographs from Sharlot Hall Museum Collection.

Sharlot Hall, c. 1920

reface

An extraordinary woman? Yes. Remarkable for her time and place, Sharlot Hall was not the tight-laced spinster her name and some of her early sentimental poems imply. She never was.

I have known Sharlot Hall for a long time. I first met her as I browsed through my uncle's book shelves on my first visit to Arizona in 1947. I remember taking *Cactus and Pine* with me to the dinner table and listening as my uncle told me of this remarkable woman whose writing had helped shape Arizona and whose persistence had established a museum to preserve history and artifacts from territorial days to the present. I mentally filed her away for further inquiry; but it wasn't until I attended the University of Arizona Graduate Library School twenty-five years later that I renewed the friendship. In a class in southwestern literature with Dr. Lawrence Clark Powell, her name came up quite naturally as we defined and explored Arizona's brief literary heritage. When I landed a job at Prescott's Yavapai College Library, Larry Powell said, "Now here's your chance. Go up there on the banks of the Hassayampa and write a biography of Sharlot Hall!" He said much the same thing to Margaret Maxwell, professor at the University of Arizona Graduate Library School, and she took him seriously. Thank goodness, for Dr. Maxwell's 1982 biography, A *Passion for Freedom: The Life of Sharlot Hall,* gave Sharlot to the public. Reading that book with its historical accuracy and human empathy not only enhanced my friendship with Sharlot, but gave me an entirely new perspective on her life.

Then, in 1984, Yavapai College granted me a year's sabbatical from my position as Public Services Librarian in which to calendar Sharlot Hall's papers in the archives of Sharlot Hall Museum. As I went through each box of writings and memorabilia, I found many unpublished manuscripts, letters, and notes which brought me even closer to the real, the inner, Sharlot. Now the friendship blossomed. Sharlot Hall became much more than the poet and historian who began a territorial history collection and founded a museum. She became the quintessential woman—energetic, courageous, multifaceted—a woman ahead of her time. A woman for all seasons.

Dr. Maxwell agreed with me that some of Sharlot's prose writings should be published. We both think that articles, letters, and spontaneous notes offer us glimpses of a Sharlot we miss in her published poetry. Dr. Maxwell's biographical introduction gives the reader the background and chronology for understanding Sharlot's experiences and thoughts as they unfold chapter by chapter.

From these unpublished writings, I have selected a representative few and arranged them somewhat chronologically. Read in order, after the biographical chapter, they document Sharlot's development as a writer and as a person. I have taken the liberty of making the changes I think she would have made before sending these pieces to a publisher. Outdated grammatical constructions, obsolete spellings, and irregularities of punctuation have been modified to fit today's accepted practice and to avoid the distracting use of [sic]. Her spelling of cañon, however, and a number of salty southwesternisms have been retained for historical flavor. My editorial comments are, for the most part, printed in italics to separate them from the body of each chapter, which is Sharlot's. I have also taken the liberty of calling her Sharlot rather than Miss Hall.

Sharlot Hall, age 16

Among Sharlot's miscellaneous papers, I found a charming unpublished verse, written in her style and her handwriting. I hope readers will agree that it makes an appropriate introduction to this collection:

With a Box of Apples

Suppose a modern Eve would come
    And tempt you with an apple,
Say just about the size of these?
    Would you temptation grapple
And manfully declare: "I won't?"
    Or, would you say: "Well, I
Think since you've picked them
    They'd be best in dumplings or in pie.
And, let us ask the serpent in
    To share with us at dinner.
A de'il with taste for fruit like that
    Can't be a hopeless sinner."[1]

Nancy Kirkpatrick Wright
1992

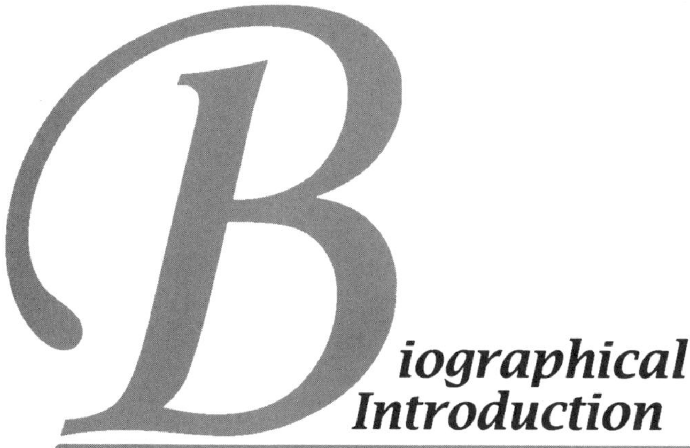

Biographical Introduction

> I am a woman a full ten years beyond thirty. I am not married. I don't expect to be married. I don't want to be married. I am happier than any married woman I have ever known. My "emotional life" is fuller in every direction than that of any wife of my acquaintance. Unless an unmarried woman is a hopeless lump of stupidity she has a hundred times wider opportunity for an emotional life full to overflowing than it is possible for an ordinary married woman to have.
>
> Sharlot Hall[1]

These words were Sharlot Hall's defiant challenge to the world. They were written out of the depths of emotional disaster which threatened to overwhelm her—but not to defeat her—during the most difficult period of her life, in 1914.

Born on the edge of frontier Kansas in 1870 to a sensitive, educated mother and a father who seems to have been almost a stereotype of the backward, unambitious frontiersman of late nineteenth-century America, Sharlot Mabridth Hall was named by her uncle, Sam Boblett. The name "Sharlot," with its peculiar spelling, was an Indian name, according to him. As for Mabridth, this belonged to a Quaker relative who had been a nurse during the Civil War.[2]

Sharlot came with her parents, James and Adeline Hall, to Arizona when she was eleven years old. James Hall settled some ten miles east of Prescott, on Lynx Creek. After several years of unsuccessful placer mining, he moved the family to 160-acre Orchard Ranch, near present-day Dewey. Here, plagued by recurring drought and occasional flooding, he scratched out a tenuous existence raising apples and pears and breeding cattle. And here the young Sharlot had time to look around her, to size up her peers at the little Agua Fria country school that she attended during the short three-month term that it "kept" each year, and to decide that this kind of life was not for her.

For Sharlot was gifted with a keen analytical mind and a way with words. Before she was old enough to write, she rhymed, and, before she could write, she learned that her love of language and her persistent queries were most likely to bring punishment and derision from her father, who looked on such activities as "high-toned." The little girl's talents were worth nothing in a world in which a woman's value lay in her ability to satisfy a man's physical desires, to produce a child "as reg'lar as the crop's laid by," and while doing this, to work harder and longer than anybody else in the settlement. Sharlot learned early that silent, seeming compliance was the best defense against masculine domination. She turned to her mother; the girl and the older woman seem to have had a bond of mutual sympathy and understanding from the beginning. But from behind her wall of seeming acquiescence, first on the Kansas frontier and next in the equally rude Arizona settlement near Prescott, Sharlot watched, analyzed, and dissected with unpitying clarity the men of her world. She concluded that "The egotism of the average man is so great that he thinks he is a glorious sight—even with a wad of tobacco in his cheek and the spit drooling off his chin." She described the world of her childhood in a succinct paragraph:

> Life was never ordered so as to give one hour for human values, human development—for being intelligent human beings trying together to get the best out of the simple routine of our lives. These poor dull old men with the wad of tobacco perpetually rolling in their jaws and the spit squirting would have stared in amazement out of their dull glazed eyes if anyone had tried to speak of such a thing. To eat, to sleep, chew tobacco, and plug along in the most

> stolid round of daily work was all they craved or could understand.[3]

The girl fought back. In October 1886, when she was sixteen, she managed to get to Prescott for a glorious half year during which she worked for her room and board and attended the new Prescott High School. Here she read, wrote poetry and essays and stories, and found sympathetic encouragement for her work both at school and in the community—for Prescott was no ordinary Arizona town; it was the territorial capital of Arizona, and a mecca for ideas and intellectual interests that were fermenting in the post-Civil War United States. At about this time Sharlot saw the first of her own words in print. The two-dollar check that was payment for her effort was nothing to the thrill of knowing that her talent had found recognition, in the world if not at home. She shared her success with her mother; her father was glad to have the money but contemptuous of "eddicated fools" who would pay for such "fine haired rubbish."

Her mother fell ill and Sharlot had to leave school. At home, she went silently about her work, feeding the calves, watering the cattle, mending harness, and helping her mother to churn, cook, and clean up after father, brother, and the inevitable hired man. But she continued to develop her talents. One of these was photography. Sharlot made many expeditions about the countryside with tripod, heavy glass-plate negatives, chemicals, and all the other equipment necessary in those days before Kodak made the whole business simple. Her photographs show an eye for composition and detail which she might have developed had she cared to pursue photography seriously. Instead, her photographic know-how was turned, as were so many of her interests, into saleable articles about the craft, articles which helped pay for Christmas gifts one year at Orchard Ranch. In addition, Sharlot became fascinated with the ancient Indian cliff dwellings which still may be seen in the remote areas of Arizona. She and her brother Ted packed in to many of the ruins in the Verde Valley area not far from their home. From these trips came further articles which found ready sale.

Sharlot, c. 1905

A series of Prescott lectures in January 1895 by the then well-known lecturer and writer on Free Thought, Samuel Putnam, drew Sharlot and her family to Prescott. Free Thought, with its tenets of agnosticism, reliance on the validity of reason as opposed to divine revelation, and its emphasis on the equality of women with men in all phases of life, found a ready convert in the young Sharlot. Heady with new ideas, she read all the literature Putnam left behind him. Before Putnam left Prescott she gave her first lecture, evidently with reasonable success, for she was asked for a repeat performance after her speech on the patron saint of the Free Thought movement, Thomas Paine.

A poem which she submitted about this time to Charles F. Lummis, then editor of the Los Angeles-based periodical *Land of Sunshine* (later *Out West)*, initiated a relationship which ripened into a close friendship with Lummis, at that time one of the pivotal figures in Southwest literature and letters. Lummis became interested in the gifted young Arizonan, invited her to visit him in Los Angeles, and launched her as his protégée into the circle of California *literati* which focused at El Alisal, Lummis's Los Angeles home (now Pasadena's Southwest Museum). Sharlot was awed and delighted with the attention; she described in naive detail her meeting with two noted turn-of-the-century feminists, Charlotte Perkins Gilman and Margaret Collier Graham. She also met Edwin Markham, Maynard Dixon, Joaquin Miller, George Wharton James, Charles Farwell Edson, Charles Amadon Moody, and other members of Lummis's circle. With many of these individuals she formed lifelong friendships.

Among the most important contacts Sharlot made through Charles Lummis was that with D. Matthew Riordan. Matt Riordan had come to Arizona in the 1870's and had worked as a miner and a Navajo Indian agent as well as owning lumber mills near Flagstaff. By the time Sharlot met him he was engineer and mine superintendent for the copper mining interests of the General Electric Company in Northern California. Until his death in 1928, he served as Sharlot's mentor, supporter, and firm friend.

Along with her Los Angeles literary work, Sharlot's star was also rising in Arizona. A product of the vanishing

American frontier herself, she had always taken delight in listening to reminiscences of the pioneer settlers of any area where she found herself. By the turn of the century she was keenly aware of the passing of the old frontier in Arizona. As Lummis was doing in California, she began to seek out Arizona pioneers, encouraging them to tell their stories. Often she would bring them to Prescott, where she introduced them to Judge Richard Sloan, himself a history enthusiast. When Sloan was appointed the last Arizona territorial governor in 1909, he appointed his friend Sharlot Hall territorial historian. He may have been surprised at the outcry that greeted this unprecedented action but he held his ground, stating that he knew of no Arizona law which would prohibit a woman from holding public office.

And so in 1909 Sharlot moved into her new office in the Arizona territorial capitol building in Phoenix. With high enthusiasm and great energy she moved forward to fill her charge—the gathering of primary source material toward a definitive history of Arizona. Traveling by stage coach, train, and horse and buggy, she visited almost every section of Arizona, even the virtually unknown and inaccessible area north of the Grand Canyon known as the Arizona Strip. She sought out early settlers as she went, making notes of their stories and collecting artifacts. She was aware of the activities of the October 1910 Constitutional Convention in Phoenix preliminary to Arizona statehood but seems to have been too busy with her own activities to take any active part in the convention's deliberations. She may not have been aware of the fact that during the course of the convention's work, some of the delegates tried to insert two planks in the proposed constitution, one of which at least might have been specifically directed at Sharlot: women were denied the vote, and only voters could hold public office. By the time the constitution was adopted, the second of these provisions had been dropped. However, the provision denying suffrage to women remained as a part of the Arizona State Constitution for some months after Arizona's statehood became a fact.

Sharlot Hall had many friends around the territory; she was strongly supported in her position as Arizona historian by the Arizona Federation of Women's Clubs as well as by hundreds of people whom she met in the course of her travels as Territorial Historian. But her popular support was insufficient to balance her unpopularity with certain key political leaders. She antagonized some of the members of the legislature. She also alienated George W. P. Hunt, first governor of the new state, by unwisely criticizing her predecessor in office, Mulford Winsor, a good friend of Hunt's. Shortly after Hunt took office in February 1912, he wrote Sharlot a curt letter, dismissing her as Arizona historian.

Not long thereafter, her beloved mother died. These two blows seem to have been too much for Sharlot. She retired to the ranch near Prescott, virtually ceased to write, cut herself off from her friends in California and Arizona, and devoted herself to the care of her father. The bleak anguish of this period and the increasingly mystical insights she attained during the last few years of her self-imposed exile she detailed in letters to an intimate friend, Alice Hewins of Phoenix. Her long ordeal was terminated by her father's death in 1925. His funeral and his burial on a hill back of the ranch were directed by Sharlot herself.

Sharlot Hall was fifty-seven when, in 1927, she signed an agreement with the City of Prescott. She was given a life lease on the Governor's Mansion built in 1864 for John Goodwin, Arizona's first territorial governor, to restore it as a museum of early Arizona history.

With the Depression in the 1930's came the opportunity to participate in federal relief projects to build a stone museum building directly behind the old log mansion and a smaller log house in the style of the little ranch houses that had dotted Lynx Creek. "Old Fort Misery," Judge Howard's original log "office" from late nineteenth-century Prescott, was moved from downtown to the grounds of the museum and set up as a pioneer lawyer's office.

In the last decade of Sharlot's life, she was increasingly bothered by heart trouble. She learned to pace her activities, to rest in the afternoon when she felt faint, and even occasionally to fend off the hordes of interested visitors, whom she still showed around the museum personally. But she maintained her keen interest in life and in the collection of Arizoniana to the very end.

Sharlot Hall died in 1943. The Old Governor's Mansion and the Sharlot Hall Museum in Prescott, Arizona, remain a lasting memorial to this remarkable woman as do the prose and poetry, Sharlot's winged words, which appear on the following pages.

Margaret F. Maxwell
Tucson, Arizona
1992

Child Life Among the Moquis

In her early notes about the Hopi, Sharlot Hall wrote, "Much has been written and said of the dance and but little of the customs and habits of these wonderfully interesting people—their religion, home life, love of children, their work in the fields—all furnish an interesting study."[1] So it is not surprising to find among her papers an unpublished manuscript in which she has written uncritically, almost lovingly, of everyday life in a Hopi pueblo. Sharlot, like most non-Indians of her day, did not know that the Hopi deeply resented the appellation Moqui, meaning "death," which had been given to them by the Spanish who first visited their mesas in 1540. They called themselves ***Hopituh****, peaceful people, which was shortened to Hopi and officially adopted by the Smithsonian Institution in 1895.[2]*

Although only a part of the article concerns children, Sharlot may have planned to submit it to ***Wide Awake****, a popular children's magazine, which had published her story, "The Genesis of the Earth and Moon, a Moqui Folk Tale," in 1891.[3]*

A brief, poignant, undated letter accompanies the manuscript:

Dear Madam;

Again I submit my notes on the Indian child-life, and with them my sincere thanks for the kindness and patience with which you have received my unsuitable manuscripts.

Very truly,
(Miss) Sharlot M. Hall,
Prescott, Arizona

A loose assemblage of notes handwritten on twenty-one small, thin pieces of newsprint, "Child Life Among the Moquis" must have been written many years before Sharlot's official visit to Oraibi in 1910. Today it is a gentle period piece:

Probably no native people of America offer a more interesting study to the ethnologist than that strange tribe known collectively as the Moquis but calling themselves the *Hanomuh* and *Hopituh.* They are the least known of the pueblo-dwelling Indians and have preserved their ancient life and customs almost untouched by modern civilization. This is largely due to the character of their home which is situated on a nearly inaccessible mesa surrounded by arid sand-plains and far-reaching deserts.

The northeastern corner of Arizona is one of the most desolate spots on earth and the little band of wanderers who elected to make a home there must have been hard-pressed by many powerful enemies. No better place of defense could be devised than these strange mesas rising abruptly several hundred feet above the barren plain and walled in by cliffs so steep that many of them stand like islets in the sea, tenanted only by the birds.

The mesa of Walpi on which the Moqui villages are located can be reached from but two points, one a dizzy trail ending in a stairway of rock where one armed man might hold back an army. Recently an easier trail has been made for the sheep and horses but, years ago, the men of old Walpi pulled up her ladders and Walpi sat like an eagle in her eyrie, defying all but winged visitors.

The Moqui still tell of one of their villages on a mesa to the eastward which was reached by a long slab of stone resting against the perpendicular wall. One summer when the men and young women were away at the grain fields an earthquake shook down the slab and left several old women prisoned in the village. They could not get down nor could their friends below reach them so they starved at their own firesides. The ruins of this village may still be traced but no one has been able to reach the mesa since the rock fell.

Hopi Village, c.1890

The very vegetation of this wild region is peculiar to itself and the human inhabitants could not but present an unusual type. The Moquis are a small, wiry, well-formed people with features more regular than the average Indian, a brownish olive complexion, soft black eyes and hair, and very small hands and feet. Many of the children and young women are really beautiful and all have a very pleasant, kindly expression.

Despite the arid soil and unfavorable climate the Moquis have always been an agricultural people. They have a tradition that, when they lived far to the south, one of their gods came and taught them the methods of irrigation which they still practice. The water supply at Walpi is most scanty but every drop is used to the best advantage and the little fields of corn and squashes yield enough food for all the villages. These have been the staple crop since pre-historic times, corn cobs and squash shells being found in the most ancient cliff dwellings and pueblos.

The ill-fated Spanish fathers who had a small mission at Walpi brought peach trees, a few grape vines, onions, and the first sheep and goats; but, though many flocks of sheep are now kept for the wool, the Moquis are almost entirely vegetarians and rarely kill any animal for food. Perhaps this has something to do with their even temper and frictionless home life. They claim that for many generations murder has been unknown among them and quarrels are so rare as to attract general attention. There is no fighting, no disputes or rough language at Walpi and some of their social usages might commend themselves to more "civilized" communities.

In Moqui-land the wife is truly queen of the home and all it contains is hers. She is always the friend and companion of the husband and "home rule" is the chief factor in the government of this small republic where there is no real chief and no officers.

But here as in the world beyond the desert is one absolute monarch; King Baby rules with undisputed power. The Moquis are loving parents and very proud of their dusky, bright-eyed little people. Perhaps they are all the more affectionate because such a very large proportion of the children die in early childhood.

The scant water supply at Walpi is warm and impure and the harsh diet of ground corn does not agree with little children. I was told that one half the babies die in their second summer and one cannot wonder at this when for long, hot months the scorching, sand-laden wind blows night and day and the only green food obtainable is a few withered onions. But for all their desolate surrounds the Moqui children are merry and bright and wonderfully intelligent.

The everyday dress of the little children is a sort of sash of red calico and as they climb in and out among the rocks and scamper along the terraced house-ledges they look not unlike a flock of fearless little robins.

Whenever a new house is built the mother sings a charm-song to keep the babies from falling off the roof, for the Walpi village is built in a very limited space and the terraced roofs form the favorite play-ground of the children as well as loitering place for their elders.

Little boys and girls play together freely but as they grow older the boys go to the fields with the men and learn to help with the planting; then they make mimic fields and hunt with little bows, and true to boy nature the world over refuse to "play with girls." Larger boys herd the sheep and ponies which have to be taken far away from the mesa to find sufficient food, and many young men cultivate little fields several miles distant.

Hopi children at play, c.1900

The women and children harvest the crops and carry the grain up the narrow pathway in baskets strapped to their backs. It is piled on the roofs and the children sort it into heaps according to color, for the Moqui corn is white, yellow, red, and blue often mingled beautifully on the same ear. Each kind is ground separately and made into the piki or paper-bread, the brighter colors being used in various religious ceremonies and given to the children on holidays.

The women grind all the corn at Walpi and the Moqui girls learn to use the mealing stones at an early age. These are large flat stones on which the corn is heaped in little piles and crushed with a small stone which is turned and twisted like a rolling-pin. The piki is a very thin batter of this finely crushed corn baked on a flat rock. The bread is baked in sheets and rolled up like paper and the girl who can make it thinnest is counted the best housekeeper.

The little girls have tiny ovens and bake mud piki and play "keep house," and often use the younger children as their dolls and babies. They have plenty of real dolls made of carved sticks dressed in gay scraps, and for "Sunday best" they have very quaint dolls modeled of clay and decorated with stripes of paint and tufts of feathers.[4]

Log Book of a Mountain Schooner

In the 1890's few Arizona ranchers had time for vacations; moreover, very few would have ever chosen to take a camping trip. However, Mr. and Mrs. John Davis planned an extended horseback excursion from their ranch near Camp Verde to the Grand Canyon and invited Sharlot Hall to go along.

Among Sharlot Hall's papers are two accounts of this unusual trip: a small tan notebook which had evidently been her journal, and a faintly penciled 125-page manuscript which parallels the journal, masking the individual people but following the same chronology and most of the same events. Her later writings show that Sharlot had a strong distaste for gossip and stories which might hurt other people. Although she saw humor and pathos in her own everyday situations, she often refrained from writing about them lest they draw attention to a friend or acquaintance.

There is no record of the Davises' original invitation or the extensive plans which must have preceded this ambitious trip. But we can assume that Sharlot had received a handwritten invitation much like the letter which introduces her fictional account:

Dear H :

We have decided to spend the summer in the mountains with the Grand Cañon as our final destination. Join us at the ranch before the tenth and bring only your blankets and clothing, as few extras as possible, and be sure to also bring a strong picket-rope and hobbles and a big mackintosh. Mr. D. says bring the biggest tin plate you can get. We've got a cook with a reputation which must be sustained, and the grub-box is over-flowing.[1]

Although the fictionalized account is engaging, with its rattlesnakes, local legends, and colorful characters, the journal's vivid, truthful picture of a nineteenth-century camping trip inspires a more lasting interest. In July of 1893, a twenty-two-year-old Sharlot Hall tucked a tan "composition book" and a few pencils in with her "picket-rope and hobbles" and set out for the Davis Ranch near Camp Verde. Here, abridged and edited, is her journal, "Log of a Mountain Schooner":

July 11. This morning our party of six persons made our start for Montezuma Well and Soda Springs. Above Camp Verde we left the river and followed the Beaver Creek road which winds over a long stretch of dreary white hills—a lime formation—very barren of grass but covered with a scant growth of Ligamum and vitae bush—perennial golden rod. Higher up we entered the cañon and wound in and out along its banks. Here the cliffs give way to hills a little less abrupt and the bed of the valley widens enough to give room for several small farms, whose green alfalfa fields contrast sharply with the barren white mesas farther back.

A ride of eighteen miles brings us to the Soda Springs—a natural curiosity of much interest. The springs are pools from two to ten feet in diameter. The water is only a few inches deep apparently and rests on a bed of reddish sand, but this sand is in motion constantly as the water boils and bubbles with the escaping gasses. The whole spring is in motion. The gas rises constantly to the surface in bubbles which break with quite a loud report. The water is so strongly impregnated with soda that a stick, small stone, or even a human body will not sink. The springs are noted for their medicinal properties and many marvelous cures are recorded from the use of the water. All the land near the springs is covered with a thick growth of vegetation and the water is drained off into a ditch and used to irrigate a fine large orchard. Montezuma Well is about three-quarters of a mile below the Soda Springs on the left bank going up the cañon. At this point of land, which at first glance appears to be a level plain, is a great round depression like a giant bowl. The walls are about seventy feet from the top to the bottom and are almost perpendicular. It is only possible to go down in a few places. In the bottom is a great pool of dark green water that sparkles and ripples, and shines like polished serpentine. The water is about eighty feet deep in the center. The current sets to the side next to the creek and there the water finds its way out through a subterranean outlet. The water can be heard falling down a ledge and the final outlet is plainly visible on the farther side. The rim of the "bowl" next to the creek is about fifteen feet across on top. But of all the curious points in the basin the most interesting is the great series of caves which have at one time formed the outlet of the pool. The Indians have taken possession of this and made their homes far back in the caves. Three have the fronts walled up with well-laid masonry and in one the corners are as neatly turned as the work of a modern mason.

July 12. This morning we made our start in a heavy shower, which, however, only lasted a few minutes. Traveled for the first few miles over a grayish formation said to be pipe clay. Then to our left we had a fine view of a spur of the red rock country—great ragged cliffs looking like castles and old English country houses.

Our road lay through the foothills of the Mogollon Mountains, a very rough rolling hill country with now and then great cliffs of volcano rock jutting out sharply from the hillsides. All this country is covered with a sparse growth of cedars, gradually growing thicker as we advance until they form a dense forest.

July 13. Drove all day through heavy pine forests with now and then a small park and some abandoned cattle ranches. Stopped for dinner at the James' ranch. Passed over the summit of a spur of the Mogollons and came at last in sight of San Francisco Mountain. Miles of fine pine logs sawed into lengths ready for the mills had been left rotting on the ground. Most of it was past use, even for firewood. In several places it had caught fire and acres of fine young pine timber was killed and the fallen timber spoiled. Camped tonight a mile and a half from Flagstaff—in a very pretty little basin surrounded by pines.

George Hance Trail, c. 1910

July 15. Stayed in camp today—had the horses shod and bought provisions for our trip. Found and pressed some handsome wild flowers.

July 16. Left camp early this morning and started to Little Springs eighteen miles away. Passed through Flagstaff which has three parts: mill town, old town, and new town. Mill town is the center of the saw mills and is now going down. Old town is set in an ugly little hollow. It is dirty and dilapidated and looks deserted. New town is laid out in crazy quilt fashion with no order whatever. It has two nice business blocks and a few nice dwellings. All the rest looks like the houses in a third-rate mining camp. Prices are very high and the assortment and quality of the goods poor. I was especially struck with the unkempt air of everything—houses, yards and streets.

Leaving the town we followed the stage road out through Potato Valley, a rather pretty, long, narrow, valley bordered by high mountains and pine forests. Here the trees have been butchered in a shameful manner. Acres and acres of great pines are sawed up into lengths ready for loading and left to rot on the ground. All the mills have been moved away and the timber that would make millions of feet of lumber is left to rot.

Potato Valley has quite a settlement and most of the land is farmed. From the hills at the head of the valley the land of the A-1 Cattle Company begins. There are several sections of land under fence and large farms and corrals. They own almost all the water and every odd section of land for forty miles.

The country was covered with a thick growth of pine trees but not many of them are large enough for lumber. The wild flowers were beautiful. We found acres of the beautiful turkey peas. They grow from six inches to two feet high and on good soil branch and form a clump. The usual colors range from pale blue to deep purple, but we found six or eight bunches of an exquisitely scented pure white variety. Mrs. Davis tells me that in all her travels she has never before seen the white flowers. We also found one bunch of a very rare pale pink variety—a lovely flower. Here we saw the first ferns, or rather bracken. It grows in great clumps and covers the hillsides. Higher up, almost on the summit of the Mogollons we came to fir and quaking aspen trees and many mew flowers.[2] We passed one small hill that was perfectly red with scarlet Indian hare bells. They grew from the very top to the bottom. They are much like the cardinal flower but are more delicately colored and have fringed petals lightly spotted with yellow.

Here also we found yellow loners much like single chrysanthemums and some beautiful flowers exactly like the Brodea Laxa. The pink wild roses are in full bloom and are darker in color than those I have seen in the valley. The pale purplish white butterfly lily is very common and very large but I have not yet seen any other color. Wild clover and alfalfa are very common.

We made camp about four o'clock, having rain for the last five miles. Camped a few hundred yards north of Little Springs, a popular outing place for the people of Flagstaff at the northern base of San Francisco peak.

July 17. Stayed in camp today and did our washing. . . . About noon I looked up and saw an animal crossing an open space about seventy-five yards north of our campfire. It proved to be a very large mountain sheep. It stopped and looked at us several times, turning broadside once. Unfortunately one of the men had taken the rifle from camp and we had nothing but a shot gun and number six shot. This mountain sheep was larger than a large deer. Its head was shaped very much like an antelope and the horns were very large—from 4 to 6 inches at the base and curled like the horns of a tame sheep.

This afternoon we visited Crater Lake, a very curious place. It is the crater of an old volcano. The lake in the bottom is fed by a hidden spring. The hill is round and not at all rocky. The side and top are covered with pine timber and the depression in the top is the shape of a wash bowl. It is perhaps a quarter of a mile across at the top. The sides are covered with pine and quaking aspen trees and the border of the water is fringed with grass and water. There are no fish in it but water-dogs are plenty.

July 18. This is a lovely morning but very cool. As cool as October in the Agua Fria (at home). Our altitude is 8200 feet . . . . We got our mail last night and I had the pleasure of getting a letter from home.

July 19. A fine day. Did not go to the lake as bears are said to be plentiful in that region and Mr. Davis was afraid we might have trouble with them. We went up on a large round sharply pointed mountain to the west of our camp. The hill is composed entirely of volcanic scoria, cinders and pumice stone of a dark red color. It is covered with a scant growth of grass and pine trees. From the top we had a grand view of San Francisco peak and could trace clearly the track of an immense snow slide on its northwestern face. To the north we had a view of the far side of the Grand Cañon—a great irregular cliff of rock looking faint and shadowy in the distance. The country between here and the cañon looks to be much more level than any we have passed over and the hills are small and set far apart.

July 20. This day opened clear and fine. About noon I took a bucket and went to the spring for water. On the way back I heard a roaring in the air like bees buzzing. Before I could get to camp not a hundred feet away, the rain was falling in torrents. For the next hour it rained, hailed, and thundered and the ground around our tents was a river. The tents stood very well although a strong wind was blowing, and did not leak at all. They were not well-ditched so a good bit of water ran under them. A perfect river ran through the fireplace, put out the fire, and almost carried away the dinner which we had on cooking. No one was much wet but one of the beds was soaked.

In the evening a curious outfit camped near us. An Indian trader and his wife and two little children and two Indians. He had shot an Indian and had to leave the reservation so he said. He paid the tribe 100 sheep, two horses, two cows and some goods. He had with him 800 sheep and a few horses and two wagons loaded with goods and wool. We went over to look at some Navajo blankets he had for sale but the price was too high and the blankets too dirty. They were a tough looking outfit and very evidently were trying to keep as shady as possible.

July 21. Cloudy today—bids fair to rain again. This is a beastly day so far—cold and windy and threatening rain every moment. We have had no good weather since reaching this place and it passes my comprehension

why people should care to come to such a place to camp year after year. The place is dirty, cold, and damp. I should much prefer to spend the time at home.

July 22. This day has opened clear and fine but very cool. Clouded up at noon and rained all the rest of the day.

July 23. Cloudy and looks like rain. I shall write home today as one of the men goes in to Flagstaff tomorrow. Rained nearly all day and a great part of the night.

July 24. Cloudy and cold. We are staying in camp closely. Have not described the trees before but will do so now. The largest are common pine—the giant so far measures 13 feet around at the foot. The fir trees are by far the handsomest we have seen so far. They are mostly small here but one near our camp is at least three feet in diameter. They are a very dark green color and an inch or more of the tip of every twig is shaded as pale smoky green. When the sun strikes the trees they are beautiful and look as if they were frosted all over.

We find here service berries, having a leaf like an elm, only more rounded and berries like a rose seed boll. The berries just ripening now and are all shades from green to black on one bush. They have very little flavor and are very full of seeds. We have found a few bushes of the thorny gooseberries. The leaves and bush are exactly like a tame gooseberry except that the leaves have a slight coarse fuzz on them. They have no flavor except a flat green acid and look to be entirely worthless, but people here say they make a good jelly. We have found strawberry and raspberry plants but no berries yet. We also find a curious poison plant called poison grape. It is from 3 to 10 inches high and looks exactly like a young scrub oak. But it bears a bunch of fruit the size and color of grapes—which are said to be very poisonous.

The quaking aspen trees grow only on the high points and extend over half way to the top of San Francisco peak. They very closely resemble a cottonwood in leaf and bloom, with pods full of cotton but smaller than the cottonwood. The bark is very smooth and looks as if it was too tight for the tree. A grove of these trees is a more ghostly looking place than a graveyard. They look at first sight as if all the trunks were thickly white-washed.

We have seen very few birds and those of but two or four varieties. The cedar bird is most common [now called the Steller's Jay]. It is the size and shape of a very large blue-jay but the color is the darkest navy blue, shading to almost black and with black markings. The crest is very large and fluffy and their voice is a most disagreeable harsh squall. I heard a flock of them this morning swearing at something that displeased them and thought they were acting very much like men on election day. They are a most beautiful bird and are only seen in the high mountains.

Little brown wrens are common and several varieties of snow birds. We have seen one flicker and one small black and white woodpecker. Hawks are very scarce and we have seen no eagles at all though they are said to be common.

The grey tree squirrels are different from any I have seen. They are the size of a very large rock squirrel and of a soft dark grey color with a pure white belly and brown markings on the back and paws. They sometimes have tassels on the ears like a lynx. They live mostly in trees and feed on young pine buds and cones and the bark on the small twigs and are not bad eating, being very much like rabbit in flavor, though very tough. Rabbits are scarce. The grey and brown chipmunks about the size of a large rat are very common. They are prettily striped on the back and are cute little animals but very full of mischief and great thieves. They are very bold and come into the camp and steal pencils, combs, spoons or any small article left in their reach. Last summer Mrs. Davis caught one carrying off her purse with fifty dollars in gold in it.

Today several parties passed our camp on the way to the cañon. One outfit was coming back. They were a party of six or eight officers of the German army. They were got up in regular tourist style and had full new outfits of saddles, guns, etc., which they had bought in Chicago.

My letters were sent out on the stage today. I cannot understand how this happened as I know no one in Flagstaff and had not spoken to the post office people.

A civet cat [skunk] paid me a visit last night and I promptly raised the camp—but his feline majesty had decamped. I did not scream or let anybody know that I was scared.

July 25. Clear today. Shall do our washing today as we move on tomorrow. Went to see Mr. Hochdoiffer and got permission to put Bonnie in his pasture. Her back is so sore that we do not care to take her on to the cañon. How good it seems to see the sunshine again!

July 26. Left camp early this morning and took the road for the Grand Cañon. Travelled for the first few miles through a forest of grand pine trees skirting the northern base of San Francisco peak. The road passed through a bit of level land bordered on each side by low hills of volcanic origins. The hills are much the shape of a large bowl turned upside down. In the top of each is a depression of greater or less depth. These craters are all filled with water in the rainy season and in a few the lake is permanent. The sides are covered with small pines and stunted cedars. They do not appear to have thrown out melted lava—but rather ashes, scored bits of pumice stone, and fine gravel or sand. The sides show no large rocks. Those usually seen are from the size of one's fist down. The soil is all of a brownish red color—like burned brick and appears to be lifeless and unproductive. There must be more than a hundred of these craters along our road. Gradually we leave the pine and come into a forest of cedars and fifteen miles from Little Springs, we leave most of the timber behind. From this point we have a view of a long stretch of barren country, round volcanic mountains and narrow open valleys extending to the Little Colorado River.

Here the ground is as bare as a floor, hardly the grass roots are left.

Passing Klostermyres we go on three and a half miles to Hull's ranch. This is a station on the stage line and a ranch of the A-1 Cattle Company. The water which we found in many long log troughs is piped down from a spring up on the mountains. Here we found that the old road to the Cañon was abandoned and, starting from Hull's ranch, there is a stretch of twenty-two miles without water. We watered the stock, had dinner, filled all our water kegs and moved on.

The country north of Hull's ranch looked very much like Lonesome Valley—a wide valley, bare of timber, bordered by low round hills and mesas, and back of them high pine covered hills. It was entirely bare of grass. To our left we had a view of Cedar Springs on the old Cañon road—and above them Red Mountain above a peculiar round, flat-topped mountain covered with trees. The soil looked as red as paint or blood. This mountain is a noted landmark and is set down on the maps of the Territory. One large high volcanic mountain, one near the Lee's Ferry road, is so deep that its crater has never been explored. We have prepared ourselves with rope and shall try to go down in it on our return trip.

We made a drive of ten or fifteen miles and went into camp—a dry camp—just at the edge of a cedar forest. We can see beyond us the far-away blue line of Coconino Forest. No large mountains are in sight as we have dropped below San Francisco and crossed a hill which hides it from view. We are encamped in a little basin where the horses have very good grass but no water except what we have hauled. All around us are small cedars. The hills are low and rolling with low wide valleys between. We are not alone as we have a family of fellow sightseers in our train. The men killed a fine mess of rabbits and squirrels this afternoon.

July 27. Left camp very early this morning. We were gradually going up grade all that time and at last the cedars gave place to piñon pine and, after passing Moqui station, to pine. This station is midway between Hull's ranch and the Cañon. The water supply consists of a large tank which is filled by the rains. After leaving the station we travelled all afternoon through heavy pine timber—the Coconino Forest. After hours of travel through this seemingly endless forest we came up on a high hill and caught a glimpse of the Grand Cañon. These views were grand indeed but we hurried on to make camp at a point where a trail goes down.

July 28. Moved camp this morning, are now in sight of the Cañon. We walked out along the rim this afternoon. The bottom usually hidden from sight is so far below us that great trees look like bushes. The point that fixed my attention most closely was a great cape or promontory, projecting out into the main Cañon. From the bottom the rocky cliff rises in five terraces, each one marked by a wall of rock-like masonry. Across the Cañon and all the way up the rim as far as we could see are great turrets and castles, peaks that might easily be mistaken for giant architecture.

The Cañon at the point where we first viewed it is 6545 feet deep. The rim is a great wall of light grey and red stone, lime and sandstone. The first wall is usually nearly perpendicular and from 200 to 1000 feet deep. Tall slender rocks stand out turret-like on the very edge and great boulders lay along the rim, seemingly ready to fall over at a moment's notice. Below this wall great ledges of red sandstone alternate with terraces of a very abrupt angle for half the distance to the river. Then come large gently sloping mesas, bearing yet the marks of the great water which made them. Below these the rocky walls begin again, granite and sandstone, and extend to the river.

Everywhere irregular side cañons cut back into the main walls—some several miles long. Between these and the river stand enormous peaks of stone washed by water and cut by wind into fantastic shapes. The giant castles with turrets and bastions are realistic enough to appeal to the most sedate mind. The poet can see wondrous visions on every hand. Some of the peaks end in pinnacles resembling statues set on a giant pedestal but the one which pleased me most is the form of a couchant lion or sphinx. This figure is probably a mile long by half a mile wide and is of a yellowish stone set on a base of dark red sandstone. The view up the river from the Berry and Cameron Trail is magnificent—the great peaks and walls of the Cañon are softened by the soft blue haze which seems to fill the Cañon.

July 29. This morning early our party of eight persons started down the Cañon. We carried plenty of lunch, three canteens full of water and a few wraps, as we expected to go to the river and stay all night. This trail, the Berry and Cameron Trail, was made as an outlet to the Last Chance Mine. It is three miles from the top of the trail to the mine. The trail starts off with a sharp descent and in places it is built up with logs and held in place by iron bars. It is well cared for and in good repair as it was only completed last February. All the water and every bit of food, clothing, lumber and supplies must be hauled from Flagstaff and then carried or packed down the trail.

The only trees are stunted cedars and small brush. On the way down we found spice wood, skunk bush, some new flowers, and a beautiful white-flowered mimosa bush. Around the rim where the timber comes up close to the wall of the Cañon we found great quantities of Cardinal flowers—scarlet and pink and a beautiful yellow coreopsis. I have never seen so much ball cactus in my life and its rose-colored blossoms were out in full force. In the Cañon we found very large cactus covered with buds exactly like cotton. These open and show large yellow flowers. We saw several varieties of prickly pear cactus and many thorny bushes whose names we did not know.

We found fossilized shells in the sandstone in one place on the rim of the Cañon and about half-way down I found a great many small shells very perfect and not petrified.

The cliffs everywhere from top to bottom show the action of water. Many places on the rim look like water-washed caves and are covered with coarse stalactites. We found chalcedony everywhere and some exquisite clusters of crystals are embedded in the lime rock on top. All along the walls of the Cañon are caves from the size of a trunk to those whose openings must be a hundred feet across. The large caves are mostly beyond reach and no one has tried to visit any of them.

The three miles down to the mine are not particularly difficult compared to that beyond. From the mine to the river it is four miles of the worst road I ever saw. There is no guard and nothing to prevent one's falling. The trail is almost perpendicular in many places and full of loose rolling rocks and shale which make travelling very dangerous. In other places it passes around mountain sides so steep that one must lean up the hill to avoid falling. The trail is very narrow—scarcely wide enough for one person to pass—and so rough that a misstep would send one hurling down the mountainside to certain death. A mile and a half of the roughest trail climbing I ever tried brings us to the bed of a Cañon. Here we find a seep of water very warm and sweet with alkali. Our canteens were empty by this time and we were glad enough to see the water—poor as it was. We found a shade under a stunted cedar and had dinner. On this part of the road we all suffered from heat. The heat in the Cañon is something beyond belief. The rocks gather and reflect the heat and the sun glares from the white formation until the air is suffocating.

There is no wind in the Cañon—not shade enough for a lizard—and no water in this trail except alkali. After a long weary tramp across cañons and over hills we came to the river bank, but were disgusted to find ourselves 2500 feet above the water. One of our party determined to have a drink from the river, followed the trail a mile farther down stream, and by very hard and dangerous climbing succeeded in reaching the water's edge and filling a canteen. The river is 300 feet wide in the narrowest point and 25 feet deep in the shallowest. The water is very thick with mud and looks yellow from the top. It is not at all bad to taste. We took fishing lines but decided not to use them as the lines were 2480 feet too short.

A tired and weary group we were as we dragged ourselves back to the spring in the side cañon. The women getting in half an hour in advance of the men. We lunched again and then pulled out up the toughest part of the trail. We reached the mine at sunset and rested and had lunch. Here Mrs. Davis and myself plotted mutiny which resulted in a unique experience. The men wished to stay at the mine all night and go up in the morning. We saw from the stiffness in our limbs when we stopped to rest that after a night's rest we should not be able to walk at all. Leaving the mine at 8 o'clock we took up our line of march up—up—up. The Cañon was a grand sight but a cloudy sky hid the moon and caused us to travel very carefully along the narrow dangerous trail.

Darkness overtook us about one third the way up and it was almost impossible to follow the narrow crooked trail. The climb was very exhausting as the grade was so great for the first mile but later on the moon raised and we had easier climbing. The trail passed out around sharp points of the cliffs where the wind struck us with terrific force and seemed to shake the cliff. The great Cañon looked full of a grey mist and the sharp points were all softened by the mist light. The walls towering over a mile above us were awful in their immensity and in the dead silence—unbroken except for our steps and labored breathing. I could fancy I heard the beating of the heart of the universe. All the spirits of the past seemed to gather here and to stand guarding the Cañon.

We were a glad party as we reached the top and dragged ourselves up to the cabin of Berry and Cameron to ask the time. It was 12 o'clock and 15 minutes. We had come the three miles with a grade of at least 2500 feet in four and a quarter hours—good time for strangers travelling in the dark. We had yet a mile and a half to make but the road was comparatively level.

We found that our weary limbs refused to move well on level ground. We had been going up or down hill so much that our walk was like the roll of a sailor.

Hance cabin at the Grand Canyon, c. 1900

We got to camp at last, had a lunch, and went to bed utterly worn out, but glad that we had put that awful trail behind us. Mrs. D. and I had also the pleasure of being the first ladies to come out by night.

July 30. Our party came up this morning and we met them at the top with a wagon. They were a tired out lot of tourists and too sore and stiff and lame to walk without groaning. We who came up the night before were as bad. We were as sore as if our bodies had been severely beaten. The trip is a terrible one and the men were fully as worn out as the women.

The going-down affects the feet and calves of the legs. Our legs were swollen and so sore that every movement was a misery. My weak back suffered much and we have a perpetual song now of Oh dear! Oh my! With a chorus of Ouch! Ouch! Such a worn-out-like party I never saw. A bear might easily corral our entire camp—not one of us is able to run.

As the bone-weary "tourists" moved from place to place along the Colorado Plateau, Sharlot wrote brief notes in her journal, including this description of Cedar Ranch, midway between the Little Colorado and Flagstaff:

It is most dreary and lonesome place yet. We found a woman, a bride of a few months, living in tents and a shelter made of gunny sacks nailed to a frame. Her husband and brother were in charge of the station.

Then, on August 10, she wrote:

Moved on to Flagstaff today. I rode in the wagon as my back is very painful. Suffered a great deal. We made camp in a little valley on the Mineral Belt railroad 2 miles from Flagstaff. Have decided to go home on the train tomorrow.

And on August 13:

Got home today—my cruise over, but the schooner will be out nearly a month more.

This memorable trip inspired several of Sharlot's poems. Some are sublime hymns of nature, others mere parodic doggerel. All of them reflect the homey, sentimental poetic styles of the 1890's. "The Wail of the Weary Eight," however, still speaks to all who have "hiked the Canyon":

The Wail of the Weary Eight

Take us up tenderly
Lift us with care.
We've done the Grand Cañon and all the sights there.
We're done up completely
We wish we were dead.
Our feet are worn out
And our brains are like lead.
We've seen the great river
As onward it flows
And beg you give ear to the tale of our woes.
We traveled over cañons and mountains of rock.
By trails that would give e'n a blind man a shock
We dared not look downward for fear we should fall
And above us the mountain shut in like a wall.

The way was so narrow like Indians we passed
And the one that was safest was he who went last
For we slipped, slid and stumbled and scrambled and
    swore
Down an incline of forty degrees or still more.
There was water, they told us, quite near to the trail
A spring that we'd find and enjoy without fail.
Well, the water was alkali—bitter and hot,
Full of wiggle-tails, tadpoles, Lord only knows what.
But we drank it for thirst was the master that time
Then praised in strong words that adorable clime.
The thermometer stood at a good baking heat
And the rocks were too hot to be used as a seat.
And the shade that we hunted and panted and prayed
    for
Well! shade's not the thing that a cactus is made for.
We were broiled, grilled and toasted, browned off like a
    ham.
Our remarks savored strongly of fool with a dam—
And one of us said as he toiled up the track

May I turn to a sheep's horn if e'er I come back.
O'er the rest of our troubles I'd best draw a veil.
Suffice it to say that the head of the trail
We reached before midnight, foot weary and sore
And tramped on to our quarters a mile or so more.
We'd took in the Cañon and owned it was grand
But next morning scarce one of the party could stand.
And Job's lamentations were nothing to ours.
We longed for down pillows and arnica showers.
For rivers of glycerin, mountains of lint,
Cold cream, porous plasters, and rest without stint.

When we next see the Cañon, we'll come to the top
Quite contented to view the whole thing and then stop.
The bottom's all right and the river to boot
But we know all its beauties by heart and by foot.
With a knowledge dear-bought in experience's school
If I go down again please just label me "fool."[3]

Roadrunner

Roadrunner

Out of the western chaparral
 Where the raw, new highways run,
He flashes swift as a rainbow flame
 And races the morning sun.
He perks and preens with lifted crest,
 He dances, heel and toe
He will jig and flirt in the roadway dirt—
 Then—off like a shot he'll go.[1]

On the back of a handful of frayed, faded newsprint pages on which Sharlot Hall had written one of her numerous diatribes against crude frontier men is an article entitled "Birds." Perhaps Sharlot intended to write several personal observations of a variety of southwestern birds—the ubiquitous scrub jay, the colorful hummingbird, or the friendly house finch, indigenous to the farms and ranches of Lonesome Valley.

***Field Guide to Western Birds** gives the roadrunner two paragraphs,[2] but Sharlot, carried on by her own momentum, added details about his nest, his voice and even his skin. Would you like to know if he would be good to eat? Even* *though the first page of the article is missing, you may learn more than you ever wanted to know about roadrunners.*

The manuscript is undated; however, a note on the June page of Sharlot's 1895 calendar, "Article on Road runner for ***Popular Science Monthly,****" was later penciled out. Her note and her fresh, unpolished style suggest that she wrote "Roadrunner" when she was about twenty-four. Here, then, is apparently the first publication of this charming evocation of Victorian folk art:*

Pea-fowl, chaparral cock, snake-killer, racer, and road-runner. The Mexicans call him *'Paisano,'* and also *corredor del camino* which equals his most common English name of roadrunner. To the Navajo Indians he owes the name of cha-cha-la-ka, based on his own harsh cry.

But roadrunner is the most apt title for he delights racing along roads and trails at a speed which protects him from all but the most fleet-footed enemies.

In appearance this small knight of the road is at once beautiful and amusing. He is about the size of a magpie but his long body and long slender, peculiarly set limbs give him an odd, ungraceful movement, a sort of hop, skip, and jump.

The head is large and surmounted by a huge green-tipped crest standing up like a helmet. The large, bright eyes full of life and fun and the bill, long and slender out of all proportion, give him a waggish air not at all out of place.

His prevailing color is grayish brown spotted with black and white, but very daintily like the breast of a quail. The back, wings, crest, and tail are a rich bronze-green with touches of blue which glistens like burnished metal in the sunlight.

The roadrunner rarely flies, for his small, stubby wings will bear him only a short distance, but given half a chance it takes an excellent dog to catch him running.

I have seen him fly into low trees when closely pursued or sometimes dart behind a clod or tuft of grass and crouch down like a quail. But he is neither timid nor helpless and can make it very interesting for a foe who ventures too near the needle-sharp beak.

This beak seems to serve as a sort of hunting spear for I have watched him thrust it through an unsuspecting grasshopper or lizard and hop off with the wriggling prey deeply impaled on the point.

The roadrunner's food seems to be mostly insects and small lizards and horned toads, with some seeds and green leaves. In captivity they are very fond of raw meat and eggs, breaking a hole in the latter with one stroke of the sharp bill and sucking out the contents. And I suspect from signs around their haunts that many low-nesting birds know them for robbers and real "road agents." They make very interesting pets and are easily tamed and cared for.

It was long supposed that the roadrunner lived mostly on the deserts and arid mesas, nesting only amid the yucca and cactus of these solitary places; but closer observation has shown him to be as partial to farms and grain fields as the bob white.

Roadrunners usually go in pairs and are quite fearless of human kind, often making their home near houses. In fall and winter the cocks run alone and are so bold one might think they had been tamed by captivity.

The nests are places in the heart of a clump of yuccas or some low bush a foot or two from the ground. I have seen one in a thick growth of willow shoots springing from an old stump not a hundred feet from a farm-house. It is a round heap of small sticks with a grass-lined depression in the center holding from two to four pure white eggs, nearly round and larger than pigeon's eggs. The nesting season is from May to July and, though the young birds are shy and rarely seen, one may hear them answering the calls of the old ones from the brush.

The voice of the roadrunner is harsh and peculiar, its usual cry being almost exactly like the barking of a young puppy. Many a time I have turned from the road to look for a puppy lost in the chaparral, only to see the flitting bronze-green back of cha-cha-la-ka racing up the trail.

The Navajo Indians fancy the birds say *"cha-cha-la-ka, cha-cha-la-ka,"* mocking the rattle of the desert rattlesnakes. The roadrunner has been more than once known to kill large snakes and to this possibility is due the superstitious awe with which most Indians and Mexicans regard him. They make him the hero of many strange stories, the following being a favorite with the Mexican children:

Corredor del camino, they say, is the hereditary enemy of the rattlesnake and never permits one to escape him alive. If he can catch the snake asleep, he strikes one powerful blow on its head with his long bill and it is all over with his snake-ship.

If the snake is awake, the hunter flutters around him until the angry reptile coils to strike. Then the bird plucks off bits of cactus and encircles the enemy with a prickly wall; after which he begins the final attack by signaling, fluttering, and cautious nips from his bill.

At last the snake, tormented by its tireless enemy and met at every hand by the thorny wall, grows furious and throwing its fangs into its own body completes the revenge of *corredor del camino.*

The reason for all this is found in the following legend: When all the animals went to the ark previous to the flood the roadrunner, who did not fancy confinement, took a seat on top.

The rattlesnake saw him and promptly told the other passengers. They called to him to come in but, as the rain was then falling, no one dared go out after the renegade. The elephant, however, reached his trunk out of the window and catching hold the bird's long handsome tail tried to pull him inside.

Roadrunner struggled bravely and freed himself—but it was at the cost of his tail. All that was left of it were three long, stiff feathers.

He kept his place on the ark and lived through the flood but his tail never grew again, and he and his descendants have kept up a bitter vendetta against snakes ever since.

Be this true or not the roadrunner has a long narrow tail which contributes much to the oddity of his appearance.

The Navajo Indians hold the roadrunner sacred to the rain-gods because the birds are seen in greatest number just at the opening of the July rainy season. They never kill *cha-cha-la-ka* nor disturb the nests except to get the feathers for religious ceremonies.

After the opening of spring the medicine reeds or cigarettes used in various ceremonies are always filled by pushing in the tobacco, herbs, etc., with the tail-feather of a roadrunner. This is to insure a wet season for the crops and plenty of grass for the stock. After harvest the reeds are filled with a night-owl feather to bring warm weather or a mild winter.

The skin of the roadrunner carefully dried with wings and tail outspread is worn as a head-dress by impersonators of the gods in the rain-dance and its cry is imitated in the rain songs.

The Moqui Indians also value the feathers highly and four of them attached to a reed a foot long are hung from the roof-beams to bring good luck and keep out evil spirits.

It is probable that the roadrunner has always been an object of interest to the peoples of the Southwest for it is found carved on various pictured rocks throughout the section.

Where they are allowed to come and go undisturbed around ranches, the cocks become very tame and one fine bird made himself much at home with us for three years. He would drive the chickens out of the yard and seemed jealous of every small bird that dared to enter his domain. One day some scarlet geranium blossoms in the window attracted his notice and he sprang up angrily against the glass and tried to tear them away. His bristling crest and flashing eyes reminded us of the proverbial "bull and red rag."

The flesh of the roadrunner is too poor to tempt any hunter, but his beautiful feathers are much in demand for ornaments and collectors place a high value on the skins and eggs, so I fear it will not be long before this interesting little knight must follow his brothers of the road into extinction.

For the present, however, *corredor del camino* is one of the oddest, most fascinating bits of life in all the Southwest.[3]

The Trip to Roosevelt

In 1905 most Arizonans would have asked, "Where's Roosevelt?" It was such a new community that only a handful of people knew of its existence, although farmers and developers in the Arizona Territory knew the importance of the proposed dam on the Salt River, northwest of Globe. They had long wanted a series of dams to control waters from the high mountains to the north, prevent spring flooding, provide timely irrigation, and generate electricity for the growing Salt River Valley.

Theodore Roosevelt signed legislation in 1902 establishing the Bureau of Reclamation, which in turn led to the creation of the Salt River Valley Project and Roosevelt Dam, the first dam to be built with federal funds. It was and is the largest masonry dam in the world.[1]

The Apache Trail, leading to Roosevelt Dam, twisted precipitously from Mesa to the new town of Roosevelt. Early in 1906 officials of the Southern Pacific Railroad, hoping to develop a tourist attraction, appointed a committee to choose names for communities and points of interest along the route. Sharlot Hall was selected to head the party making a preliminary trip up the Apache Trail before deciding upon "authentic and appropriate" place names.[2]

I was called at five o'clock and, after breakfast in the stuffy little hotel with the suggestive name of "Alhambra," left Mesa at six—long before sunrise. The big Concord stage rumbled up to the door, drawn by four horses. One glance inside and I asked permission to share the driver's seat in front—high up above the horses. Under my feet were piled two sacks of potatoes, the mail sack for Roosevelt, and half a dozen small way-sacks of mail for little mining camps and stations along the road.

Construction workers at Roosevelt Dam site, 1905

It was still quite dark when we started. Mesa was hidden in dim tree shadows and only an occasional dog or rooster lifted his voice. The muddy road lay dark and rutted ahead, with pools of water from the late rain shining dimly all along.

The driver gathered the lines in his hand, swung the long whip in a big circle that ended in a sharp pop like the crack of a pistol shot, and with a lurch and roll we started. The mud clung like wax to the wheels, and the stage worried along from side to side of the road, vainly hunting better going.

As it grew lighter I saw the great, level valley in which Mesa stands—flat as a floor it seemed in every direction. Long lines of trees, dark and still, outlined the farms. The houses were dim bulks of shadow and the cattle in the alfalfa fields were still asleep in groups. The broad Salt River Valley grew in every direction with the light, and the farms and town were only a dot. Camelback and its kindred peaks grew purple and red and the low bulk of Mt. McDowell glowed a deep and deeper red-purple with pale, thin mountain masses in receding lines of many-shaded blue beyond.

The great, saw-toothed crown of Four Peaks swung out in front, blue, cold, snow topped, and straight ahead the huge, turreted bulk of the Superstition Mountains stood brown and wild and mysterious with the long, dark muddy road running straight toward it.

The stars grew paler—Venus hung like a big pale lamp in front and a faint, thin crescent of late moon was tangled in the web of cloud across the East. Pale red streaks began to come and the shallow pools of water along the road held the flecks of cloud and the dying stars as farther back near the farms they had reflected the tree tops. We passed wagons loaded with hay, their breakfast camp fires just lighted, the pungent smell of the wet road coming along with us into the desert.

Cactus began to mingle with the mesquite and creosote and palo verde, but as yet the road was over a level plain and the vegetation was not profuse or tall. The road curved to the left and neared low hills. Then rank on rank the stately saguaros appeared growing taller and thicker as we went, intermingled with ocotillos, great groves of tall mule opuntias, many-branched buckhorn cactus, fishhook or bisnagas, big and little. The palo verde trees grew taller, the mesquites thicker, the catclaw more tree-like. And the road wound into pocket-like green thickets where the arms of the giant cactus almost touched the stage.

Now the road was the one built for the traction engine which brings crude oil from Mesa to Government

Wells from which point it is hauled in tank wagons by eight-mule teams into Roosevelt. The road is broad and new and very good but because of the rain and deep mud the traction engine did not attempt to leave the shed at the Wells.

We changed horses at a small place near Goldfields—a semi-deserted mining camp that had promised more in the recent past than it is likely ever to fulfill. It lies at the foot of the Superstition Mountains. To the right the main peak of the Superstitions rises, a strange splintered mass of bare rock thrust up like jagged teeth against the sky. The top of this mountain is set with sharp spires of rock like a forest of broken tree trunks standing black and sharp against the sky. There are but two ways to the top and up those the Apaches used to retreat with their stolen herds of cattle and ponies when pursued on their way from raiding the Gila and Salt River valleys. Al Sieber, the old scout, says that the top is still covered with the bones of horses and cattle killed and eaten there. It was at the foot of this mountain that King Woolsey's famous pinole treaty took place.[3]

Beyond the great mountain the road entered a tangle of foothills and cañons and began to climb a well-made grade over a rugged backbone capped with rough red sandstone. The cacti and desert shrubs continued in profusion but the beauty was of the earth itself—the red browns and dull yellow and tawny gold of the cliffs and rocks.

On the narrowest part of the grade we found an oil team of eight mules and two heavy tank wagons stalled in the mud. For three-quarters of an hour we were held there while the men and mules tried to move the big wagons into a narrow curve in the road where we could get past.

At Mormon Flat we had a swift view down into the cañon of the Salt River—a grand cañon not dwarfed of dignity because its dark-seamed cliffs were something less tall than those of the great Cañon of the North. Here we crossed a deep gully by a well-made bridge and rolled up to the little station—a mere handful of tents—where we were to change horses. Two women and two small children came out to watch us and ask eagerly for the mail which was in one of the little way-sacks for them. The camp was on a little flat and on all sides the great hills and cliffs rose up and shut them in. It seemed a lonely and remote place shut away from the world as with walls of iron.

The new team swung into the road with a plunge as the two men at the station let go of the bits of the leaders, but the driver was a horseman of tried skill and under his hand they came down to a long, steady trot and took the long grades evenly.

The road wound over such a tangle of cañons and mountain tops as made the breath stop. It was a maze—now down with a sweep through some swift stream bed, and up and over a knife-like "hogback" between two deep cañons, where the bottom lay dim and dusky hundreds of feet below. As we advanced on a steady trot it was like skirting the brink of the Grand Cañon and threading in and out among its many-armed side cañons. From the very edge of the roadway, not three feet from the wheels, the cliffs dropped down straight and sheer 500 feet and more. Chipmunks darted into cover and birds flitted in and out, but we had left the rabbits, big and little, down in the lower desert.

Higher and higher the road wound till looking in all ways we were encircled by succeeding ranges of bare blue mountains, sheer and cañon-cut and uptilted as if it were a stormy sea turned in full tide to waves of granite and sandstone with curling foam crests of limestone in dull white and gray. Below had been some formal placing of peak and plain. Here on the crest a hundred mighty peaks and ridges and then a hundred more were flung in lavish confusion—an intricate, infinite sweep of rolling mountains, blue and bluer to the dim cloud line. Now draped and hidden by clouds and long gray lines of rain which were lifted and flung back and forth in the uncertain wind.

By a road like a very maze we came to the top of a great backbone and looked down 600 feet into a cleft of green cañon with boxed walls of rough rugged sandstone across which it seemed easy to toss a stone. The sheer walls broke straight down till they were lost in shadow and over them the road dropped like a rope swung over a cliff.

This was Fish Creek Hill, a road whose like is not to be found in the Territory if at all in the Southwest. A drive to the bottom of the Grand Cañon would be longer, but it could not be more beautiful or exciting. Broad—that is with three feet to spare beyond the outer wheel—smooth and extremely well made, the road sweeps around walls and angles turning corners with astonishing sharpness and hanging above dizzying depths till the eye loses sense of distance. Above, the dark cliffs are red, brown, and a deep, dull green, streaked by wide black water marks where little streams brought by the recent rains fall down. Some of them were still dripping threads of silver. Others were dark shining streaks along the wall. Below was Fish Creek Cañon—a deep, dim, lonely place widening out at last to a lower cañon but still grand. At the station we got the fourth team and our belated three o'clock dinner—and went on.

The hills grew lower and the road, climbing over them, dropped down along a chain of granite gravel hills to the bank of the Salt River and took its way along the stream—a graded roadway only a few feet from the water.

For miles as the horses kept the steady trot the wide copper-red river, muddy and swollen, rolled on one side of the road and the cliffs rose high and brown, cactus covered and rough on the other.

It was cold and the rain fell in misty sheets along the top of the cañon and down the mountain sides. The sun had been hidden for hours and the driver was hurrying to reach the grade leading to the town before night and darkness. The cañon shut in again and from the river's edge we began to climb the red-brown grade that wound up the sheer hillside. Up, still at a swinging trot, around the brink of a cañon dizzy almost as Fish Creek Hill with a sheer wall for a hundred feet we dropped down from the road edge over a great rock-spur through which the road had been cut by sheer force and held up by the highest unmortared wall in the world. The great gap of the town site and lights of the town of Roosevelt came in view. We saw the dam site as from a narrow shelf far up the mountain side above it. The brown rock-ribbed walls with their strata of red sandstone slanting upstream at a sharp angle like the shut jaws of some stern mouth and the dark, muddy, copper-hued water slipping between.

Mail wagon on Fish Creek Hill, 1905

Beyond, outspread like the great wings of some bird, stretched Tonto Creek and the Salt River winding down from widely distant sources to meet a few hundred yards above the dam site. Far up both streams the water shimmered in the dim light and the lights of the town on the right and the contractor's camp on the left shone out.

The stage driver turned into still other shelf-like roads along the mountainside till he stopped on the hill where the engineers have their homes and left me at the house of the superintending engineer.

It was a dark, cloudy, storm-threatening night and I could see little, but in the morning from the porch I had a wonderful view. The camp is on the right shoulder of the cañon perhaps 300 feet above the river. Below and across like a great panorama lies the basin which will be a lake when the dam is built, its two great arms reaching back into the mountains till the view is lost in the tangle of blue peaks and ranges.

This is the heart of the Apache land of old—from the Superstition mountains eastward to the head of both streams. . . . The government has bought these ranches and on one of them raises hay, melons, vegetables, etc., for the camp. They will all be under water when the dam is completed and filled.

Looking north from the dam site the stout, broad bulk of Dutch Woman's Peak faces the cañon gap already being blocked with raw, new, quarried stone. . . . The camp here is a comfortable and well-arranged tent-village, over which the stars and stripes float above the small blue flag of the local reclamation service with its white swastika in the center.

The valley has the sweep of the outspread wings of a bird so the lake will be like a silvery blue heron or a great gray eagle along the rugged hills. The town of Roosevelt will lie under water and the nearest foothills will be islands with rolling rounded backs rising out of the late-born lake where nature seems to have planned from the beginning to make man her partner in creation.[4]

Alone: The Essential Sharlot

> Cease to mourn; thou hast thy memories—but for me Krishna decreed no friend—and though I wander all the worlds I am yet alone.
>
> Sharlot Hall[1]

Sharlot Hall needed no psychologist to tell her that loneliness is not dependent on the externals of person or place, that indeed one can be the most desolate when surrounded by other people. The theme of lonesomeness occurs again and again in Sharlot's writing, often quite naturally because the mines and ranches described in her stories and articles were remote and isolated. Her letters, essays, and poems frequently responded to friends' concerns about her personal isolation and her chosen unmarried state.

We know that Sharlot had at least one great love, the lecturer and Free-thinker, Samuel Putnam. However, little of the correspondence between Sharlot and Putnam has been found, and Margaret Maxwell's meticulous research for the biography of Sharlot Hall failed to completely clarify the relationship. Sharlot met Putnam while he was in Prescott in January of 1895 lecturing for the Free Thought movement. He quickly developed a friendship with the Hall family and soon Sharlot was also speaking on Free Thought to local groups. She corresponded with him during his lecture tours in the East and in England. Within a year, however, word reached Prescott that Putnam had died from escaping gas fumes in a Boston apartment. Newspaper reports of his death revealed that a young woman who was traveling and

Sharlot at Orchard Ranch, c. 1900s

lecturing with him died at the same time. Even in his late fifties he could charm young women with his courtly attentions and his anti-religious, free-love philosophy. Sharlot's poem "Alone" was probably written soon after his death:

> . . . What know you, though you grieve,
> of loneliness,
> Who count the days back—sure of smiles
> that were—
> And eyes that looked and loved and under-
> stood?
> Empty the arms, companioned still the soul—
> For souls once met blend all futurity
> Into that meeting . . .[2]

The several interesting people she met while in California working for Charles Lummis's ***Out West*** *magazine in 1905 eventually disappointed her. It was her first extended time away from Lonesome Valley and she wrote in her diary:*

I find it vastly more comfortable to trust no one—but be kind to all and give them as much courtesy and outward friendliness as may be—while keeping them inwardly so far distant that no thing they do can hurt me much. A selfish thing, perhaps—or would be if I did not give lavishly of kindness—but to live at all one must have some wall between one's heart and the world—and it is better to be a little lonely behind the wall than to stand the target of many arrows outside. In truth I have been vastly better able to help people and make things pleasant for them than would have been possible had I cared much about the whole matter myself.[3]

Sharlot's essentially religious and philosophical nature reveals itself in a letter to Alice Hewins twenty years later, beginning as usual, "My Dear Girl":

. . . Because the poems helped you to pass the week I am going to write you a little letter that, I hope, may help you when days seem lonely—for someone may have told you that all my life has been much alone.

You will know, as I do, that being lonely is not because we are away from people, or because we are with them—it is something that people have nothing to do with—(though quite often we think they have a lot to do with it).

This feeling of loneliness—and of undefined aspiration—is really the deepest self within us reaching out and trying to touch the Infinite Creative Power and to be part of it. It is like a little drop of water trying to remember the ocean of which it was once part and to which it will return. It is not a sad thing but a glorious thing—connecting us always with that Unseen as if we just reached out a hand in darkness and took sure hold of Infinite Safety.

We are never so truly ourselves—nor so truly "In tune with the Infinite" as when we are a little out of the world of Everydayness. At first it scares us and makes us feel helpless to be all alone with ourselves—but soon we know that no soul really lives any other way—it is always the Infinite and our own souls alone with each other for each one of us, no mere human being can come very near to us.

It is true that the poems you like best express the feeling we all have of longing for and seeking out the "Perfect Comrade"—that feeling is part of our growth—it is Growth itself, forcing us forward into the infinite by making us feel a great lack and emptiness in the life of the moment.

At first we think that somewhere there is a human being who could fill all that loneliness, satisfy all that hunger for a larger and fuller life, give us strength to do great things and to live greatly. In every beautiful thing, and in every new human being we meet, we seek that source of greater strength and clearer inspiration, and the pleasure of being understood and encouraged. Sometimes we live a long life and do not learn what it is that we really seek. Each person and each condition disappoints us no matter how sure we were at first that this was the end of "The Long Quest."

I know now that I was very fortunate in being born in a wild and unsettled country where I met very few people, had very few books, and had to realize very early that the "Perfect Comrade" was always with me though unseen except by my deepest self.

Living far from other homes, from towns and cities and all social life, I soon found that none of these were necessary to growth or happiness—that they were good and delightful to have but that they were not even the beginning of "The Long Quest"—for that was a thing between the Unseen Infinite and the deepest part of myself.

Sharlot And Alice Hewins at the ranch, c. 1924

I came to see that the love or friendship of a demi-God could not make me either larger or smaller in my own soul—that no human being could make me of true worth except myself. I came to know that the greatest love anyone could give me would not stop the hunger for that comradeship with the Source of Life—the creative urge out of which all life comes.[4]

Sharlot Hall, c. 1918

Spring in the Desert

According to Margaret Maxwell, Sharlot Hall's biographer, "Heavy rains fell in January and February 1905 all over Arizona; as a matter of fact, the year 1905 holds the record as the wettest year overall in Arizona in the past 400 years.[1] But though the resulting flooding of the Salt River wreaked havoc in the Phoenix area, the wet winter meant an unusually beautiful spring in the desert. By this time one of the editors of the well-known Los Angeles-based periodical, ***Out West****, Sharlot gathered her note pad and went south to see the spring and to write about it for* ***Out West****. Written in the anxious days preceding the congressional debate on joint statehood for Arizona and New Mexico, Sharlot's article was designed to introduce Easterners to the desert as it actually was—not a shifting desolate Sahara-like waste of sand dunes, but a green, colorful, and ever-changing land whose fragile ecology depended then as now on chance rainfall."* [2]

Spring in the desert—not a thing of calendars nor of precedent. No man can say when or even where it will come, for it is sometimes as much a matter of locality as of season. It depends upon what the winter has brought, and that may be (once in a decade) long, steady, soaking rains; thunder showers with all of summer's artillery; flying squalls of sleet and snow and hail, swept down from the distant mountain tops on the wings of a winter hurricane; or just endless days of sunshine and drought.

If it is rain in any quantity, the very drops seem to turn into green leaves as they fall—and, almost before the shower is done, a faint, gauzy film of green, like a scarf blown from the hands of Spring, lies on the canyon slopes and along the wide, low sand-washes.

Every little herb and weed and tuft of grass makes haste, with the inherited instinct of a hundred drought-scourged generations, to be its utmost in the shortest space of time. Before the first leaves have half unfolded, the eager bud is thrusting up with unswerving determination to fulfill its life in advance of the ill winds that are sure to blow.

By March of a rainy winter the valleys are golden with poppies, tall and thick as wheat, and long splashes of blue and purple lupines sweep up the hill slopes and down the cañon sides, mingled and brightened with orange-scarlet and blood-red "Indian pinks." The alfilaria, or "filaree," far wanderer from Spain, lays a thick carpet underfoot, starred with thousands of tiny rose-red flowers and sending up a pungent herb-sweetness when crushed under shoe or hoof.

And yet in all this fragile, swift-passing beauty the real things of the desert have no part. It is their working season; they are busy storing up the uncertain moisture in leaf, or trunk, or root, for the drought that is always ahead. Their color deepens and freshens, but not till later will the blossoms come; from the middle of May till the last of June the aristocracy of the desert hold their brief court.

Not first in coming, but first in stately beauty, the Giant Cactus (*Cereus giganteus*) forms its long, thick buds in early May and opens them in June—crowns of carven pearl on the top of every huge limb. The flowers are not more than four inches across and are shaped like the familiar prickly-pear blossoms but their heavy circular clusters, high on the branches, make the cactus forests look not unlike white-capped armies marching up the long ridges.

Hummingbirds revel then, poising like flame over the snowy blossoms; and wild bees swarm and buzz and gather the thick, white honey that is often stored in a cavity of the great trunk of the very cactus from which the sweet was stolen.

At dusk the flowers have a strange, sweet, intangible fragrance in keeping with their other-worldly beauty.

Sharlot in desert, c. 1910

While the Giant Cactus was only turning a deeper green along its flute-ribbed columns, the many-stalked, slender, whip-like ocotillo, the "fish-pole cactus," was busy fringing its full length with small, light-green leaves—real leaves in texture and habit, to be taken on at the coming of moisture and dropped precipitately on the approach of drought. Each whiplash branch-tip is weighed down by a cluster of buds, unfolding the most graceful of all the desert cactus flowers, soon to open in long pendulous fuchsia bells of richest red.

The low, rough hills beloved of the ocotillo blaze as with a thousand uplifted torches through the June days, and later the withered flowers hang like clots of dried blood.

Desert dwellers cut the ocotillo into convenient lengths and plant it in close rows for fences—that often grow and blossom in red glory for years to come.

The Opuntias, big, shaggy, rough-branched fellows, some of them taller than a man, and known variously as "candle," "buckhorn," and "mule" cactus, make whole corners of the lower desert valleys and cañon bottoms gay with their blossoms varying through shades of yellow from greenish lemon to golden, with some varieties a rich magenta red, golden-hearted and sweet.

And whole mountainsides are yellow at once with the deep, rich, velvet-textured prickly pear, mingled in a few localities with a thinner-leaved, less thorny variety, covered with exquisite rose-red flowers like crinkled silk.

After them, flaunting from high clefts in the cañons and rocky hillsides, the many-flowered *Echinocereus* feels the spring in its blood and greets it with rosy or crimson or yellow banners. The baby "fish-hooks" with their wire-like, tiny, curved thorns become veritable bouquets, and the tiny, round balls of white thorns no bigger than an egg, or a cluster of eggs, cover themselves with wide, rose-red sun-hats, as it were.

The "desert water barrels," the *Echinocactus,* "fish-hook," or "bisnaga," as they are variously called, are slower. They show a scattering crop of blossoms in June, but a few weeks later each one will wear a golden crown. It is from the smaller of these plants that the Mexicans make a much prized sweet, not unlike candied pineapple in appearance.

Sharlot warily approaches cactus, c. 1910

The very spirit of the desert, surpassing almost the Giant Cactus, the great tree-yucca lifts its tall white cluster of waxen bells like a flag of truce to the Sun God. No other desert growth is more impressive than a great yucca in full bloom. And when in and out among the yucca forest, the Giant Cactus rears its white crown and the strange, pale-green palo verde tree spreads its lace-like leaves and showers of golden blossoms, the desert is indeed a garden and holy place.

Every desert shrub and tree has its own spring-song, translated into leaf and flower and sweet odors for the enlightenment of duller souls. No cherry tree of Japan is more fairylike delicately exquisite than the palo verde in its spring robe of golden frost flakes, and no lilac was ever sweeter; though in this there lingers a haunting strangeness, like the wild beauty of untamed places.

The ironwood, friend and companion of the palo verde, has its own honey-sweet, locust-shaped blossoms; and the pale, fringed, inconspicuous mesquite flowers are heavy with fragrance. Even the creosote, the resinous "greasewood," takes a still brighter gloss to its varnished leaves and veils itself in delicate yellow blossoms.

Spring in the desert goes on all summer. If no rains come between January and March, the small things sleep and wait. The cacti and yuccas, noblesse oblige, keep their truce with June, but cautiously, not lavishly. The shrubs blossom a very little, with like caution. Then, if July spills her largesse of "summer rains" down the mountain sides and sweeping through the long dry cañons and washes of the desert everything wakes up in haste to make the best of the delayed spring.

Perhaps one rain-swept valley will be green and flower-strewn, while another, a few miles away, neglected by the Capricorn's "thunder heads," will lie as brown and dry and lifeless as in midwinter. One side of a mountain, shower favored, may be green as a meadow, while the other is desolate and brown.

When this brief, late spring comes like "St. Martin's Summer," strange whims take the desert things; the mesquite blossoms a second time, and bears another crop of the beans that are bread to the Indians and food to all the desert animals. Many of the cacti put forth another crop of blossoms, fewer in number, but larger and more rich in coloring. Even the fruit trees in the little ranches along the edge of the desert blossom a second time in August, or even September, if the rains come.

While the cacti tryst with June in the lower deserts, the barren foothills and desert mountains hold nooks where the smaller yuccas, the "Bear-grass," and "Adam's needle," and "Spanish bayonet," and the tall queenly mescal, make a wonderland of strange, almost uncanny, beauty. The mescal, a rosette of strong, thorn-edged sword-shaped leaves, has stood for a dozen years perhaps, widening slowly year by year till it covers a space three feet across. Then some spring calls resistlessly, and a big, blunt bud parts the thorn-ribbed heart and starts skyward.

Six inches or more a day by actual measurement, pale green, rose streaked, ribbed and flecked with gold like some great oriental flower, it keeps its upward way; ten feet, fifteen, twenty if chance favors; and the bud opens into a many-branched cluster of flower-buds, not unlike the tree yucca, but of a deep, golden yellow flecked with red. Then the bees and birds revel; orioles leave their valley nests and scold the hummingbirds away from this rich banquet. Flies and moths and all honey-lovers gather as by special invitation, and feast where the stately flower sways in the wind.

But the mescal does not always come to this maturity. When the desert spring is at its newest, little bands of Indians, usually the women and children, seek out these favored nooks that have been known to their ancestors for generations, and have a great "mescal bake." The heavy bud is cut just before it emerges from the thorn-ribbed leaves of the heart, and piled up in stacks like some new kind of cabbage.

When enough has been gathered—and the gathering may go on a week or more—a big hole is hollowed out in the earth and filled with wood and flat stones. The wood is fired and burned to coals; then the pit is cleaned and the mescal laid in, covered with the stones, more wood, and sometimes earth. The baking lasts three days or more—and when the pit is opened, even the passing white man does not disdain to feast. Near every mescal thicket will be found the old baking pits half obliterated by time.[3]

CHAPTER SEVEN

The Unmarried Woman

Men. By the time Sharlot was in her forties, she had seen enough downtrodden women and unhappy marriages to cause her to look upon the masculine gender as a pretty sorry lot—with very few exceptions. When she said, "I am happier than any married woman I have ever known," she meant it. Furthermore, she spoke and wrote pungently on the subject as few women of her time dared. When a women's magazine questioned women's ability to be emotionally fulfilled outside the marriage tradition, Sharlot fairly bristled. Here are excerpts from her unpublished response:

> Possibly I got an overdose of matrimonial felicity from those books which had grounded my grandmother's mind in the principles by which she lived till my grandfather put her name on a sightly tombstone and proceeded to install another victim before his household altar—or maybe it was merely the daily life of the married woman whom I grew up with—anyway I began to size things up at an age when my girl playmates were beginning to dream of dark-eyed heroes—and the result was like a pail of ice water over any budding tendency to romance.

Seriously and sadly—the average husband is a tough proposition out of which to get any satisfactory "emotional life," and the average mother never gets time for any real life with her children after they are out of her arms. There have got to be wives and mothers—God bless them and give them the crown of martyrs! But don't waste any sympathy from them by handing it over to the unmarried woman.

Emotional life! I wish I could print it in double caps. What married woman ever has a chance to have a fine honest friendship with any man but "Him"? She doesn't know what friendship means, even with other women—she hasn't time—and if she had, "He" would be jealous before it was fairly started.

My beautiful mother never knew any man but my father beyond a speaking acquaintance in her whole married life—and my father was much more interested in his livestock and farm than in her tastes and desires. Her "emotional life" was confined to one man whose chief interest was whether she had dinner ready—I have fine, wholesome friendships with a dozen men who don't care whether I can boil water or not. I share their work and play and problems and thoughts as my mother never had a chance to share with anybody, and one and all they show me a consideration which no "Noble consort" of my experience ever showed to his "Companion."

I speak seriously—no married woman dares to know well in genuine friendship any man except a blood relative. Seldom indeed has she the chance to get any man's viewpoint on life but "His"—and he invariably edits his opinion down to her level of understanding.

I, one of the women denied an outlet for my emotions in husband and children, have more homes than fingers into which I am warmly welcomed—where the children come to tell me their troubles or share the wonder-magic of youth's dreams which "Mother" is too busy to understand; where "Mother" comes to ask about how the children can be set safely on the high

The Hall family, 1905. L. to R. Mrs. Adeline Hall, Edward, Sharlot, and father, James

roads of life—roads which I, not she, have mapped and charted by travelling over them.

An unmarried woman with good hard sense and sympathy can touch dozens of young lives to help and inspire; she can draw to her a circle of young men and women that will outlast her life. The best friend in the world for a boy is an older, unmarried woman who has sense and sympathy and a fine code of honor. . . .

I am no genius, no beauty, have no "accomplishments" and I live on a lonely country ranch—but when chance sent me here I went out and adopted all the young folks in the community—and the old ones too.

Any woman who isn't a fool will find life warm and full and fine flowing all around her; husband and children, other women's homes, her own work, all these are mere incidents—*life* is bigger and fuller and finer than all these—they are good; take them who may; but *wake up*, not *pity*, the woman who thinks that any one, or all of them, is *life.*[1]

CHAPTER EIGHT

Lonesome Valley: Sharlot's Southwest

An immense valley stretches south from Seligman past Prescott almost to Humboldt, Arizona. In the early days winter snows often covered the grassy plain, and trees grew only on the foothills of Bill Williams Mountain and Granite Mountain. The first wide prairie was Big Chino, named for the high curly grass, described as belly-high to a tall horse, spreading to the hills and beyond. The broad, flat basin narrowed into Chino Valley, and finally squeezed between Mingus Mountain and the standing boulders of Granite Dells, flowing past old lava-plugged Glassford Hill (Sharlot Hall's "Bald Mountain"), finally becoming Lonesome Valley. Orchard Ranch lay on the edge of Lonesome Valley, and Orchard Ranch was Sharlot Hall's home for almost forty years. The ranch was about five miles from the farming-ranching community of present-day Dewey and perhaps fifteen miles by winding wagon road east of Prescott. The area was sparsely populated in the 1900's, growing to no more than fifty families in the 1930's.[1] Pictures of Orchard Ranch show a two-story board-and-batten house surrounded by a spiked fence and then a sprinkling of chaparral vegetation on the surrounding hills. A windmill rises starkly at the rear of the house, with a few outbuildings and trees barely relieving the harshness.

Orchard Ranch in winter, c. 1890

In her twenties, Sharlot kept a notebook she labeled "Phrases, Hints, and Odds and Ends of Thought," in which she recorded her reflections on friendship and love and religion, along with a miner's prayer, notes on breaking horses, maps to local mines, and an enchilada recipe. Here she first wrote of Lonesome Valley:

> Lonesome Valley—as bare and brown and lonesome as its name implies—and as beautiful as only the southwestern plains can be—dappled with little hills and marked by long sweeping lines of color as rich and bright as if some titan painter had just drawn his wet brush down the rolling slopes.
>
> Vegetation is not needed to produce beauty in this land for the earth herself is many-hued—streaked with strange bright sands and clays and walled with mountains of rich-hued rock.[2]
>
> Bald Mountain—not a kingly mountain—just a human one, scarred over with the trail of dead fires and

having all sorts of deep lines that recurring sorrow brings. It is like some great soul that burned with love and hate and ambition and all the rest till there is no fire left—but everybody stands a little way off—afraid of what the scars say but the lips never tell.[3]

And I myself may well be the desert mesquite—thorny—stubborn to knife and axe, hiding half its growth in the silent sand, and schooled to long endurance of shifting wind and burning sun—poet-hearted facer of difficulties that yet keeps heart to blossom for the wild bees and birds.[4]

We know there were times Lonesome Valley lived up to its name, especially during the long years between the death of her mother in 1912 and of her father in 1925.

The winter of 1913-14 was a grim one for Sharlot; it had snowed before and after Christmas and the continued sense of loss after the death of her mother would have filled a lesser woman with waves of self-pity. The light irony and humor of her post-Christmas letter to her trusted friend, Alice Hewins, only hint of her heavy heart:

The minute the sun began to shine I took to the hills and my New Year housekeeping has been a fright. . . . However, my birds do quarrel, even right on the porch roof where I feed them crumbs. I am coaxing all the wild things near—as long ago when I used to be at home—owls, squirrels, quails, roadrunners and blue jays [Steller's jays]—my mixed up family. They almost walk over me when I am lying under the trees out in the hills. . . . The cold days I spend in a big upstairs room where I have a stove and am very comfortable with the funniest old tag ends of long discarded furniture and boxes . . . and evidences of my genius like the typewriter table. . . . My birds fight just outside the window. . . . Mr. Riordan sent John Muir's "Autobiography" which is fine, and E. S. Martin's new book on the unrest of women[5] which is gentle mild trash . . . . I take refuge in the hills when I can endure this house no longer.[6]

By February the long winter of cold and isolation began to take its toll on her good spirits, and Sharlot finally responded. Her response was characteristically Sharlot—get to work! So, she fought the mental and physical isolation of Lonesome Valley winters with activity, and her next letter to Alice was filled with news:

> The neglected boys at Dewey, with no place but the saloons to go to, got on my nerves so that last week I rounded them all up, filled them to the teeth with pumpkin pie and organized them into my own particular "gang." They are regular little toughs but no one ever tried to make them otherwise, so they can't be blamed—and I've promised them a picnic on the 22nd and a picture show on the 28th—and you know I can't break my word to them. I guess no one on earth ever played fair with them so far. . . . Then I rounded in the women—about as hopeless a bunch as you ever saw—and started the "Friendly Improvement Club" and that has strings on me too. But Alice, their need is so great—only God knows the dull life . . . and I got a smashing compliment from one of the boys. He rounded up a chum and made him help wash the dishes and as we talked he said, "You bet we'll have fun —you are just like a boy." I've got to live up to that, of course.[7]

In May she wrote Alice describing an Easter picnic with her gang of boys:

> We had a big crowd but they were just the greenest ever—awkward as a bunch of range cattle in an alfalfa field. . . . I had coffee and a huge pyramid cake over two feet tall with little toys and things hidden in every slice—lots of things to make them laugh—and I tell you, dear, the jokes have to be mighty simple and plain too.[8]

Those interminable years in Lonesome Valley finally passed, of course. The intrepid Sharlot survived and she eventually began the life of historical stewardship she had long envisioned. In 1928 she wrote Tim Riordan, brother of her good friend, Matt :

To sort of bridge the years I will say that even before father's passing the old ranch was slipping back surely, and sadly, into desert—indeed all the surrounding region was slowly reverting to the lonesomest sort of "Lonesome Valley" and many of the old ranches were deserted.[9]

Lonesome Valley was left behind, spiritually as well as physically, and satisfying years of fulfillment and purpose lay just ahead.

Working on the tack at Orchard Ranch, c. 1900

Carlos Parra

How Splendid Is Our Past: The Mansion

I believe the truth of what I once heard Calvin Coolidge say that we are not prepared to live well in the present, or to shape the issues of the future, unless we know the past so well that its ideals and inspirations are still alive to us.

Sharlot Hall [1]

Sharlot Hall celebrated Arizona history abundantly. She collected memorabilia and talked about her vision of a historical museum when she traveled throughout Arizona as territorial historian from 1909 to 1911. At meetings of the Pioneers Association, she urged the old-timers to save "everything," and to write their stories so they would not be lost. Finally in her mid-fifties it looked as if her dream of a home for her ideas and her collections would become reality. Her beloved mother and her crotchety, difficult father were both dead. She was free. At an age when many women of her day were admiring their grandchildren, nursing their aching bodies, perhaps indulging in a bit of harmless gossip, and becoming ladies of leisure, Sharlot was tackling her most formidable project—the restoration of the first territorial governor's house and the founding of a museum. Her active commitment to preservation was to last the rest of her life.

Archivists at Sharlot Hall Museum have compiled folder after folder of letters congratulating Sharlot as she acquired the Governor's Mansion and began remodeling it. Well-known statesmen, as well as old personal friends, sent heartfelt responses to the news of her inspiring project. Governor Hunt wrote, "I was very glad to learn that you have accepted the responsibility for preserving the old house of the Governor at Prescott. The task could not have fallen into more capable hands." [2] *Other supporters offered artifacts, help, and money.*

It was a project whose time had come. In 1927, Sharlot wrote to J. Andrew West, Prescott city attorney, outlining her plans for the mansion:

> Twenty years ago I wished to buy this old building from its owners and preserve it and make of it a museum and historical library for Prescott and Yavapai County—but the necessities of my home life prevented.
>
> Since the building came into the possession of the state and under the custody of the city of Prescott, I have tried frequently to find some way by which my original purpose might be carried out—but without success.
>
> During that time many of the best collections . . . things of priceless interest to Yavapai County early history have gone beyond recall. . . . I wish to be sure my personal collection will never be moved away from Prescott—either in part or in whole—and that the museum and historical library purpose will be carried on after my death.
>
> I wish absolute freedom to finance the work in whatever way may seem best as it develops. The beginning must necessarily be very modest and limited.
>
> I wish absolute freedom to develop the land around the building into the most beautiful park possible—in time—and to place upon it whatever buildings or objects may be in harmony with its original purpose . . . . I expect to make my home in the building for such

time as that may contribute to the development of the museum plan and the care of the objects assembled.

I hope to make this building and the grounds around it a center of historical and literary interest and a sort of civic center for the pioneers of Yavapai County and for such organizations of young people as might be benefitted or inspired by its ideals and purposes.[3]

The Governor's Mansion as Sharlot first saw it, c. 1880s

Records at Prescott City Hall indicate that the city council acted quickly, giving Sharlot a life lease on the Mansion and grounds. Sharlot was already making specific plans: [4]

Slowly I am going to restore the old house to its past and refill it with things in harmony with its history, and the history of our beginnings as city, and county, and state.

I am going to do this just as I can—first a new roof, perhaps a roof of pine from our own hills, just such as the first governor sat under. Then a strong fence around the whole plot of land—which is to be someday a park of native Yavapai County shrubs, plants, and wild flowers—and also the site of the most picturesque mining exhibit ever brought together, in Arizona at least.

My fingers itch to pull off the rustic which in October of 1899 was nailed over the old logs. I hope to find them well-preserved underneath. . . .

I want to get under the layers of cloth and wall-paper and see if any of that costly (original) lumber is left—if it is, it is all going to be exposed to the eyes of every visitor. . . . and I want to "claw off" all the stuff that has been put over the ceiling beams year by year and see how they look from below.

As the old house is made over I want to gather into it every object of interest in reach connected with our past—old books, old pictures, old furniture that came to Yavapai in covered wagons—old cooking utensils—all the homely things of our everyday life when railroads were far away.

One room is to be entirely for things of the old cattle range—spurs, bridle bits, real riatas, and "McCartys"—stirrups, saddles. The kitchen, which was only a stockade of posts set on end when the first wedding supper served in Prescott was cooked there, will be filled with homely old cooking things and china and glass beloved of some of our pioneer women—and the bedrooms will have patch-work quilts on them . . . .

I have enough things of my own collection to make a mighty fine start—and when all of my things are settled in the old house they are to belong to the people of Prescott and Yavapai County "forever and ever, Amen." And I believe that from every corner of the county will come other things of historical and pioneer interest to be preserved along with them for future generations of Yavapai people.

My friends say to me: "How are you going to finance it?" . . . And I say: "It will finance itself in the start—everybody will want to help a little for sheer love of pioneer days and the Old West that now only lives in a few places like Yavapai County. If I am willing to give all the rest of my life, all my work and all my time—and all I have when I die—for the "Old Governor's House" has been made my legal heir—then I know that enough for the beginning will come to my hands—and once the gates are open to visitors the Old Governor's House expects to . . . become an endowed institution out of its own revenues.[5]

As the restoration got under way, Sharlot soon realized she needed some expertise as well as some unusual materials. She wrote Timothy Riordan of the Arizona Lumber Company in Flagstaff on her newly printed stationery:

Miss Sharlot M. Hall
The Old Governor's House
Prescott, Arizona

Dear Mr. Riordan:

. . . I had gotten from the city of Prescott a life lease on the old log house variously known as the old capitol, the old Fleury House, and the old governor's mansion.

The poor old house had stood alone and neglected for many years—outwardly it was like an old tramp—who certainly hadn't "Used Pears Soap," or any other—for many a year. Most people said frankly that I was crazy to take it, or want it—and real estate men were all in favor of pulling it down and putting the land to some modern use.

The city fathers were glad to get it off their hands and so they threw in electricity and water along with the dirt and decay—and wished me well in financing it the rest of my life.

I moved in in March—with the water pipes busted, light wires too dangerous to use . . . . I pulled a ton of tacks and got the old cloth and paper off the walls and ceiling—and then I heated water in coal oil cans on the old fire-place in the governor's office and with homemade soap I tackled the soot and dirt of sixty-four years.

For some weeks I was the color of the soot all day long—and I tried out every variety of scrubbing brush in Prescott—in fact I held daily court mounted on a long carpenter's trestle and entertained visitors while I scrubbed ceilings.

The mayor called on me, and though he is a garage owner and fixes the insides of cars with his own hands, he backed off from shaking any hand as black as mine—and I could not blame him.

. . . While I was cleaning up the inside I had a man patching the roof, which looked like a net to catch the stars—and by way of diversion the front steps fell off and the back windows fell out—but at last the old wreck looks like a human habitation—and to my great joy we find the old logs sound right down to the ground.

Eventually we will dare to strip off the weatherboarding and restore the logs to light of day—but the first "got to have" is a roof—and if it is practical I wish that it might be a "shake" roof as was the first one.

That brings me to . . . ask if you ever cut shakes, or split them, in your lumbering . . . . It may be that shakes are more expensive and I must do all the repairing at the least cost as there is no fund of any sort for the repair or upkeep of this old building.

So far the material used has all been from the ranch or from the old place itself—the cost has been nearly all labor and I have met it myself. . . have spent about a thousand dollars and I believe that at least two thousand dollars worth of work has been done—and all of it so well that it will stand for many years—perhaps another sixty-four.

Former estimates for the restoration of the place were never under five thousand dollars—but half of that will work wonders.

My plan is to go as far as I can and then stop and earn again, and go on.

The city of Prescott is bound by the lease to take care of the old house and its contents after my death—but I am left quite free to determine the character of the restoration and use during my lifetime. I want it to be a center of inspiration in a finer citizenship—a center of the finest memories of the past.[6]

In August of 1928 she again wrote Riordan, thanking him for donating materials. She included some of her down-to-earth philosophy of museum development:

This isn't a high-brow museum—it's a place where all sorts of old household things, early tools—the rough things with which the first lap of the wilderness was conquered will find their place. I care for things of human use more than for the rarest art detached from daily life—so you can guess what collections these old logs will presently cover.[7]

All was not smooth sailing, of course. Sharlot became ill, and, on top of that, neighbors objected to her new fence. She met both problems, characteristically, head-on:

Governor's Mansion during Sharlot's curatorship, c. 1940

I am out again as bold as "Buckey O'Neill at San Juan Hill"—and ready to say "The job was never invented that can keep me from doing some more work if it's needed—work can't kill me." . . . Really it's a lot of fun—all this planning to make one dollar do the work of ten—and to use old materials and odds and ends from the ranch.

Did I tell you that I had almost disrupted Prescott by putting a stockade fence of mixed cedar and pine poles around the place? With the promise of some real ranch gates to be added? The dissenting votes came from some cheerful bootleggers on adjoining land whose deliveries had long been made over my land—and they stormed the city council with loud demands that I be "abated."

They were told by the city attorney that I had both an iron-clad lease and an iron will and was a nice lady to let alone—but I am waiting for their next move—they are three Texas Guinans of mature years and wide reputation.[8]

Sharlot won. The fence stayed up, and it remained there until several years after her death. During her lifetime other structures were added: Old Fort Misery, a small log building, was moved across Granite Creek to the Museum grounds, and a typical ranch house was built. The Rock Building (now called the Sharlot Hall Building), completed in 1936, provided a comfortable apartment for Sharlot and housed more artifacts.

Sharlot Hall was always willing to interrupt her restoration work to speak with interested groups, especially young people, on the value of local history to future generations. She might have been describing herself when she wrote:

So the muse of history, she of the thoughtful eyes and wise and tender face, must teach us how splendid is our past and how great should be our pride in it—and how great lies the responsibility upon us to be worthy of it.[9]

Called to the Mat

"Mat, on the—up for trial (from late 1890's) hence, in trouble (ca. 1915). . . the small square mat on which the accused soldier stood in a barracks orderly-room."

Partridge, *Dictionary of Slang and Unconventional English*[1]

Sharlot was usually too busy to take part in local politics, but she occasionally had a personal interest in city and state government. A deeply caring person, she could become righteously indignant when democratic processes or human rights, especially her own, were denied. Maxwell's biography traces Sharlot's brushes with the political system, from her 1906 efforts to block New Mexico-Arizona joint statehood to her 1909 bid for the office of territorial historian, continuing through her appointment as a presidential elector in 1925 and her break with the Republican Party in 1932.[2]

Although she was successful in her bid for a legislative clerkship in January of 1907, Sharlot's diary records tart metaphorical observations on the members of the Council of the Territorial Legislature:

> Men are always amusing and pathetic—never more so than when they are going gravely about some public business. I am finding already in the body the fighters, the diplomats, the timid, the aggressive, the lion and the lamb—and the jackal—the eagle and the barnyard fowl—and the buzzard.[3]

In 1909 Sharlot was appointed territorial historian by the last territorial governor, Richard E. Sloan of Prescott. However, as fate and politics would have it, the first state governor, Democrat George W. P. Hunt, replaced her in 1912 with his friend Mulford Winsor, who had been historian for a brief time before Sharlot's appointment.[4] Fighting to regain

Office of the
Governor of the Territory of Arizona.
To all to whom these Presents shall come, Greeting:

Know Ye, That reposing special confidence and trust in the integrity and ability of Sharlot M Hall I, Richard E. Sloan Governor of the Territory of Arizona, in the name of and by the authority of said Territory, do appoint her to be Arizona Historian. To succeed Mulford Winsor and do authorize her to discharge, according to law, the duties of said office, and to hold and enjoy the same, together with the powers, privileges and emoluments thereunto appertaining, until the legal termination thereof.

In Witness Whereof I have hereunto set my hand and caused to be affixed the Great Seal of the Territory of Arizona. Done at the City of Phoenix the Capital this First day of October in the year of our Lord one thousand nine hundred and nine.

By the Governor: Richard E. Sloan

her position, Sharlot pulled out all stops in an open letter to the legislature, describing Mulford Winsor as a man who failed to keep records, who lost manuscripts, and whose office was an unorganized mess.[5] The newly elected Governor Hunt lost no time in responding. "Frankly," he wrote, "I do not commend your taste, nor admire the spirit evidenced by your letters. . . .

Your gratuitous strictures . . . are improper, indelicate and misplaced." [6] *And that was that.*

In 1925 the Republican Party sent Sharlot to Washington to deliver Arizona's electoral votes for Calvin Coolidge and Sharlot sat in the august halls of our nation's Congress for the swearing-in ceremony. While in Washington, she wrote the Prescott Monday Club, the oldest women's club in the state, the usual descriptions of beautiful, elaborate gowns and colorful military and diplomatic uniforms in the gallery. Then she turned her attention to the legislative body. Vice-President Charles (Hell 'n' Maria) Dawes as presiding officer of the joint session called the meeting to order, and our girl of the Golden West once more lapsed into cattle-ranch similes:

> He is a tall, thin man with sharp, thin features and a particularly long nose—not a very good-tempered-looking man and quite evidently a very nervous man, at least just then [he delivered a veritable diatribe to the Senate]. . . . It was a sharp and bitter attack upon the rules of debate and procedure. . . .[Dawes] became most fierce and passionate. . . . The outraged senators looked exactly like a bunch of wild steers suddenly cornered by a rough-riding cow hand. . . . I could almost see the shake of angry horns, and lowered heads, the front feet pawing the dust before a charge, and imagine the angry bellowing of a herd ready to stampede.[7]

Her 1925 Washington trip led to a most unexpected aftermath seven years later, in October, 1932. Only she can tell it with the proper innuendo, sarcasm, and western bite.

> We all get a jolt now and then and mine came when I was peacefully washing dishes after feeding the men who are helping me to clean up the Miller Valley and the Pioneers' Home graveyards—and little did I dream that my own political graveyard was so near.
>
> From force of habit I was registered to the Republican side—since the present law requires us to have some brand for the primary round-up—but I had never felt the swing of the party riata and I expected just to

just to go on voting for the best people in sight according to my own sorting of them out.

However, though I didn't know there was a Republican Headquarters in Prescott, there really is—and it had been "keeping cases" on the doings of even as unimportant a person as myself. . . . Hence came a messenger from that headquarters suggesting that my conduct of late had been such as to call for a reprimand.

Hastily, I searched my mind for some misdeed—I had stayed at home nights; I had faithfully cared for the relics—I had met all visitors in as nearly the manner of a lady as is natural for me—wherein was I at fault?

Soon it was made clear—I had been seen in public with a lady who now holds office in Yavapai County—a lady elected by the opposing party [8]—and thereby I had given some Republican voters the anxious fear that I might be supporting her instead of the party nominee.

"Party loyalty," it seems, demanded more circumspect conduct from me than from some others because in 1924 I had been selected as one of the presidential electors of Arizona and had later had an interesting trip to Washington—for which it was now up to me to pay by so behaving myself in public that I would stir up no doubts in the minds of possible voters as to whether I might not think some candidate of the other party better fitted to hold certain office—and by supporting them by word or action.

Again I hastily searched my mind—Alas, yes! Some weeks ago the lady in question, a present office holder, had business in a region of old-time ranches which I longed to visit in search of old spurs, bridle-bits, early farm tools, and the like. I have not of late been well enough to drive my own car so far and my relic-hunting tendency was like a mountain flood long held in check by the new Banning Creek Dam—it was ready to burst all bounds of prudence and forget party obligations.

Sharlot poses in the copper dress she wore to carry Arizona's votes to the electoral college, 1925

The lady said, "Come along—glad to have you." I went—and now I know what it is to be "called to the mat" and get "called down" because I wasn't behaving properly after having had that trip to Washington.

In truth the men of the Republican Party who put my name on the 1924 ticket . . . forgot to tell me that all the rest of my life I would be under obligations of loyalty to accept any ticket put out—even so small a fragment of the party as a county list of candidates.

They had just said indulgently: "Nonsense, of course you can leave the ranch long enough to go to Washington—we aren't afraid but what you'll know how to behave in front of a president."

But that was 1924—and most of those men who had confidence in me are dead—and it seems to me the party of that day is not as alive as it might be—and the present party evidently knows that it can't trust me to pay for a "dead horse" by voting for all its selections for county offices.

So I "went to the mat"—I went up those stairs, (after hunting around to find where the headquarters was) still a gentle lady, as I thought. I came down those stairs a red hot independent—with the branding iron of insurgency on me for life.

I was the maddest I have been for many years—and getting madder every minute. I was no lady—and I am not a lady yet so far as voting is concerned. As I came downstairs I made myself a political litany—and I have been saying it over and over since like a confession of absolute faith in church at Easter.

This is part of it—and I'll stand back to the wall and be shot at by all the political guns in the United States before I'll change one line of it.

No political party can do my thinking for me.

No political party can line me up to vote for anybody that I don't believe is fitted to fill the office they are trying to get.

There "ain't no sich animal" as party loyalty which obliges me to vote for anyone I think unfit.

. . . Of course—being a woman, and no longer a gentle lady absorbed in collecting ancient relics—I added a postscript, which is always the important part of any woman's letter. It goes this way:

I will vote exactly as I please.

I will campaign for anyone I want to—even though they be a candidate of the Democratic Party.

If any voter is misled because of my conduct it's just too bad for him—because even though that trip to Washington is *not* going to be paid for—it is just too bad that the party happened to pick a natural outlaw to send to Washington—but I'm not to blame for the party's mistaken judgment.

And yet I am sincerely and deeply grateful for the honor and the pleasure and the opportunities to learn much of public life which that trip gave me.

Today I am a better citizen of Yavapai County because I have been "called to the mat." If I live and have the health, I'm going to make a lot of new history along the line of fighting against many impudent evils in state and local life and no party is going to be in position to tell me not to be seen with a friend of a quarter-century standing just because I might give some timid voter a wrong impression.[9]

Sharlot was almost sixty-two when she took on the local Republican headquarters. Age had not mellowed or tamed her observations four years later, when she wrote:

An old cowman said to me lately: "Folks are like a trail herd of cattle—the leaders and the drag never get within bawling distance of each other . . . and maybe the leaders is hangin' out their tongues with thirst when the tail-end of the drag is just pulling their feet out of the mud and climbin' the near-side bank of the last river you crossed." Another wise man handled the same truth this way: "Mankind is a marching army that has never been able to bring up its rear. . . ." And so we go—all strung out from Adam to Einstein—all trying to live in 1936—with our individual desires and capacities reaching back to Columbus—or back of him to the dawn of some pre-historic day.[10]

A Bit of Picturesque Western Profanity

"Life ain't in holding a good hand—but in playing a poor hand well."[1]

Sharlot Hall's collection of Arizoniana includes epitaphs, jingles, aphorisms, and colorful examples of western dialect as well as relics and artifacts. The picturesque words and phrases she collected were not just notes filed away for future reference. Sharlot frequently used them in her everyday speech, especially when riled, and added them for local color to much of her writing.

When Erna Fergusson, a writer of bold and colorful pieces about her own New Mexico and the Southwest, visited Prescott on her 1939 sortie through Arizona, she interviewed Sharlot Hall at the "Governor's Palace." Imagine Sharlot's showing her southwestern soul-sister the Museum and its collection of territorial memorabilia, walking from room to room, picking up cherished relics, telling stories about each one as she passed it tenderly from hand to hand. Miss Fergusson, in her straightforward way, sized up Sharlot:

> To me, Sharlot Hall was an infinitely more important experience than any quantity of old furniture, branding irons, prints, and even books. For no more Sharlot Halls are being produced, and no book will ever convey the living feeling or the true importance of this one.[2]
>
> . . . Manner, voice, and enunciation were of a correctness not often met, but without pedantry. When she needed a racy word or provincial expression, she used it with the finality of a Dr. Johnson admitting it to the English language.
>
> "Yes, the pioneers stuck together all right. They knew they'd better, or they'd be planted."
>
> Miss Hall seldom smiles, but when she does, light travels across her strong, rugged face slowly, from eyes to lips.[3]

Not only did Sharlot feel free to use western expressions, but she collected them all her life. Scattered among her papers at the Museum on scraps of paper, in ledger books and memo pads, are lists of colorful words and pithy phrases she picked up as she talked with old-timers throughout Arizona and California. Most of these expressions are listed in a small maroon record book labeled "A Round of Dialect and Word Study, Begun Dec. 1898, Sharlot Mabridth Hall, Orchard Ranch, Arizona." They are entertaining and revealing. Most are printable:

"Bogue"—verb, "to come bogueing right along," to hurry or force one's self along where not wanted.

"Dab right-down"—to come upon quickly. As in "A hawk dabs right-down on a chicken."

"Fine-haired"—as in "Oh, you're mighty fine-haired," meaning particular, refined, different from the common, above the common. Used derisively—with sarcasm and mocking. Very commonly used by people of humble origins in speaking of some one of better birth.

"Fit-i-fied"—afflicted with fits, capricious, frivolous, uncertain or temperamental.

"Fogo"—used in [the] West and Southwest in sense of a cloud. As "A perfect fogo of dust. A great fogo of smoke." Also in [the] sense of trouble or confusion. As "You have stirred up a pretty fogo." Also in sense of dusk—darkness—as "I can't see in this fogo."

"Old Poke-easy"—a term of contempt for a slow, worthless person or animal, especially a person of idle, shiftless habits.

"Scrunts"—dwarfed, small.

"Shaller-do-round"—a short jacket like a sweater.

"Skeet"—skeets right along. Slides or moves along easily.

"Slimpsey"—limp, as a garment lacking starch. Thin, sleazy material.

"Sloomsey"—ill-fitting, limp.

"Swizzle around"—to flatter and get your way dishonestly.

"Using around"—as deer using round a spring, or a man paying attention to a girl, to frequent, resort to.

"Whiggin keg"—buttermilk jar kept for making bread.[4]

Sharlot added her own definitions to these phrases:

"As fine as a horse's eyebrow"—very fine, accurate.

"Doin's around it an' gravy over it"—any extra sauce or unusual dish.

"If you harrow what I plow, you'll be tired by night" —or "you'll do the biggest day's work you ever struck."

"Knock a skillet full of hell out of you"—a bit of picturesque western profanity.

"A short horse is soon curried"—meaning that a task begun with scant means is soon accomplished, as a meal is quickly gotten when there is little food to be prepared.

"Wear all to stifins"—"nothing but stifin"—worn all to strings. The membrane around the bones, or between internal organs.[5]

Make your own comments on these; Sharlot offered none:

"Clear as a bell and cold as hell and dark as all damnation."

"A December fog will freeze a dog."

"Quick as hell will scorch a feather." [6]

She also included a counting-out song and an interesting cure:

Bee, bee, bumble bee
Sting a man upon his knee—
Sting a hog upon the snout—
And I'll be dogged if you ain't out!

To get rid of warts and styes, according to an old German cure, you must see two men riding on one horse.[7]

What are "Arizona strawberries"? Sharlot defined this western delicacy in a speech to the Arizona Pioneers Association, delivered, evidently, about the time the Pioneers' Home was being built. Her notes on "The Old Hassayampers" are a rich lode of Arizoniana:

The Old Hassayampers

The anticipation of a home for Arizona's Hassayampers, those old pioneers who lighted her first camp fires and blazed the first trails across her deserts and mountains, leads us back in memory to the days when to the average Hassayamper home meant a log cabin under the pines, a fireplace full of pitch logs, and rose-colored dreams of the girl he left behind him.

The Hassayamper was a pioneer of pioneers (for the reason that they were nearly all from other territories). His religion was to be a man among his fellow men. There were no churches, courts, schools or towns in the country in his day—every man was his own doctor, lawyer, preacher, blacksmith and judge of good whiskey.

The latch string of the Hassayamper cabin was always on the outside and his home was a home to anyone who came his way. And if we could know that he would feel as happy and as welcome in the new Pioneers Home as he made others in his little log cabin, it would be worth in satisfaction to the Arizonians [sic] of today, many times the money it will cost.

It might be that in that old-time cabin home he had nothing to offer but a pot of Arizona strawberries—the brown beans—or some venison jerky, but you were welcome to what he had and it was the universal rule that a crowd of Hassayampers would hang a man quicker for refusing to eat beans than for stealing a mule.

There were two things from which you could not separate the true Hassayamper—his sack of brown beans and his burro—and I here move that when the new home is built and occupied, a pot of brown beans be kept always boiling on the fireplace and that the back yard be fenced off to accommodate the gray and saddle-scarred remnant of the old pack trains—the faithful burros who in their humble way were as true Hassayampers as their masters and had no small part in making the Arizona of today. Someone has said that Arizona was built on beans, booze, burros, bailing wire, and horse _ _ _ _—the booze is a libel on our own glorious Hassayampa water—but gentlemen, I ask you to drink, standing, a toast, to the true pioneer of Arizona—the old Hassayamper—his beans, and his burro.[8]

No doubt the pioneers listening that day felt that Sharlot Hall deserved a standing toast. Her sprinkling of a bit of western profanity once again demonstrated that common touch which had made her a sought-after speaker and a treasured friend.

Wind Song: Sharlot through the Eyes of Her Friends

Wind Song

Free winds that wander up and down
The weary hills of earth:
What call like yours can sorrow drown,
Or touch her seas to mirth!
Strong winds that were tempestuous souls,
O brothers, turn and wait;
Take up my longing on your wings
Till I shall master fate.

Take up my longing on your wings,
O brothers, as you go;
The dauntless soul within me sings
That mighty hymn ye know:
Kindred are we, though but for ye
The boundless ways were made
Yet I would go my lesser road
As strong and unafraid.

Sharlot Hall[1]

" 'Wind Song' is much like Sharlot Hall herself," [2] *Sue Abbey, Sharlot Hall Museum archivist, concluded in her lecture on the life of Sharlot Hall. Sue's lectures reflect an almost mystical communion with Sharlot developed over the years as she cataloged the letters, notes, and memorabilia accumulated at the Museum.*

Audiences listen attentively and sympathetically as Sue begins quietly, "I like her very much. I think that she is a unique, fascinating lady and I'd like for you to meet her. She was a most sensitive woman, an aware person, a womanly person. She was a woman ahead of her time. She was beautifully expressive in her writing but inhibited in expressing personal feelings, and only a few were privileged to see the inner person." [3]

Another "real Sharlot" emerges from the writings of friends and associates who came to know her during her seventy-two years of abundant living.

When Ida Davisson, Sharlot's childhood friend, wrote her "Memories of Sharlot" in 1946, she turned back to the year 1886 when Sharlot worked for room and board with a Prescott family, in order to attend school in town:

> The first day of school was always a happy one for me, but the first Monday in September 1886 was an unusually happy one. A new girl at school! Not only new, but she was a little older than I, so it flattered me to have her notice me, and though very quiet and shy, she had a sweet smile and friendly way. So began a friendship that lasted a lifetime. I think her last letter to me was addressed to "Dear friend of all the years." . . . I think the teacher we had that year had much to do with training Sharlot in elocution. He was a young man (C.S. Gleason) who came to Arizona to teach that year as a stepping stone to being a lawyer. He was so full of pep and sarcasm. When we made a mistake we expected to be held up to ridicule before the class, and I can still see poor Sharlot cringe as he criticized her. . . .
>
> School was out late in June those days, and as the days grew longer Sharlot would often take the Adams children for a walk south on our street toward the old reservoir. I would often join her; we would sit in the shade of a tree while the children played; she would once more recite poetry, and I just "ate it up".[4]

In 1912 when A. M. MacDuffee of Chloride was collecting signatures on a petition to continue Sharlot's position of territorial historian, he wrote her, "One man says, 'Oh! that Lady who was here last summer with the two Arabian horses and tons of energy? Yes! I'll be glad to sign it!' " [5]

Sharlot's close, lifelong friend Matt Riordan wrote her from New York in 1910, "Each one of your letters gives its fresh, new note of joy. As Mr. Westover [an acquaintance who lived in New York] said the other day when we were talking about you behind your back, you appear to write as a bird sings; by the grace of God." [6]

Alice Hewins, perhaps Sharlot's dearest friend of all, wrote in her brief "biography" of Sharlot:

> Sharlot was particularly gifted to tell the women's side of pioneer life. Her warm sympathies, her gift of expression and having lived most of her life under pioneer conditions particularly qualified her.
>
> Wealth, rank or position never had any effect on Sharlot. It was what the person really was that interested her. She really was two people. There was the woman of genius, accustomed to meeting all sorts of folk. This was the woman I knew best and the people of the Territory knew. The other side which was so long the only side her home community knew and which may have had its reaction on her in her later life was the dry land farmer, peddling her produce, wearing shabby clothes and mingling with other farmers, looked on as a little bit queer. . . . I remember once when I was a girl her telling my mother she was the only happy married woman she knew, an exaggeration I felt then and still do. She really enjoyed and felt more at ease in the company of men.[7]

Sharlot and Alice Hewins, c. 1910

Grace Sparkes, Secretary of the Prescott Chamber of Commerce, redoubtable champion of Prescott and Yavapai County, and equally staunch Sharlot Hall supporter wrote:

> She had a brilliant mind. . . her serenity, her kindness . . . her wonderful philosophy. Realist—yes! For her early life had been a tumultuous one. . . . She had a deep knowledge and interest in all forms of plants. Even so-called weeds were in her sight beautiful and useful—if we just knew and understood the purpose for which they had been created. . . . There was a wonderful humorous side to Sharlot too. . . Kindness! Understanding! Yes, she could be determined with a finality that meant FINAL. . . . She was reticent when it came to her own accomplishments.[8]

*After visiting Sharlot in 1939, while on a gathering trip for her book **Our Southwest**, Erna Fergusson, herself a south-western native, wrote Sharlot:*

> No, you didn't fool me any. I know your type too well to be taken in, the really sturdy independence, and the inability to see that changing times made changes necessary. It's a type I love and respect and you need never try to impress others. You'll just naturally impress anybody who knows a real human being when he sees one.[9]

*The Reverend Charles Franklin Parker interviewed Sharlot just before her death and was so enchanted that he wrote this perceptive and sensitive word-portrait of her for **Arizona Highways:***

> Sharlot Hall is a historian, a gatherer, recorder, and interpreter of fact of people and times. She is an analyst of human nature and behavior, and an accurate reporter of events. She is a philosopher of merit and has insights into lives of persons, nations, and eras. She is gentle and forthright in her attitude and has great reverence for truth. . . . She has an excellent outlook upon all life and an humble spirit regarding her own accomplishments. . . . she told me laughingly, "I hope it will not shock you, but of all my poems I think I like best a little one you may not have even noticed, called 'Cash In.' " In this poem one senses a fatalism, possibly a slight cynicism, but in it a sportsman-like determination to enjoy life and to drink the last drop from the cup.

Cash In

O life is a game of poker
And I've played it straight to the end;
But the last chip's down on the table
And I'm done with the game, my friend.

The fire in my blood it flickers
Like a guttering candle light,
When the tallow beads in greasy tears
And the wind whips in from the night.

The deck was stacked by the Dealer
Before he would let me in;
The cards were marked, and I knew it—
There was never a chance to win.

But I bluffed the game to a finish—
Till He nodded and called my hand—
Palms empty and crossed—but the lips
  still smile—
And the Dealer will understand.[10]

Sharlot and the Reverend Charles Franklin Parker in front of the Governor's Mansion, c. 1940

Acknowledgments

This book could not have been written without a sabbatical from Yavapai College and the support of family, friends, and professionals who shared my belief that some of Sharlot Hall's prose should be published.

Mac Harris, director of Sharlot Hall Museum, gave the project the focus and momentum it needed to move to completion. Jean Cross, Dawn Dollard, Kathryn Herrick, Joan Spenser, Ken Kimsey, and many other members of the Sharlot Hall Museum staff and board of trustees offered encouragement and recommendations along the way. Jane Raymer's frank comments and critical attention to grammar and syntax solved many problems with the initial manuscript.

There would be no *Sharlot Herself* without the wholehearted support of Sharlot Hall's biographer, Dr. Margaret F. Maxwell, professor of the Graduate Library School, at the University of Arizona. Dr. Maxwell's historical integrity and her sensitivity to Sharlot Hall's life and ideals enrich this work, and her introductory chapter conveys the background and perspective necessary for a full appreciation of Sharlot's writing.

In 1984 Sharlot Hall Museum archivist Sue Abbey gave me a table and space in the Museum library and granted me unlimited access to Sharlot Hall's papers. She later proofed my manuscript and was invaluable in selecting appropriate photographs and illustrations. She guided the project through two museum directors and the board of trustees, and worked with the artist. Because I recognize Sue's genuine respect and affection for Sharlot Hall, I especially appreciate her forthcoming contributions to this project.

I wish to thank Carlos Parra who saw the humor in some of Sharlot's stories and animated them with delightful illustrations.

Heartfelt gratitude goes to Pat Jacobson who critiqued the manuscript several times with the sharpest mind, eyes, and pencil west of the Pecos. When Sharlot Hall and I liberally expressed our penchants for hyphens and dashes, Pat Jacobson considered each of them in a fair-minded and evenhanded way—allowing each of us as many as she could, while gently brushing away many others. Pat spent countless hours going over each version of the manuscript, making corrections and offering tactful suggestions. I am deeply indebted to her.

From the beginning, my friend Joan Zumwalt of Flagstaff offered helpful criticism and reassurance.

George Fuller, James B. Hopkins and Bonnie O'Dailey of Graphic Impressions shared my desire to honor Sharlot Hall with "a little gem of a book." *Sharlot Herself* owes much to their talent and attention to each important detail of designing and printing.

As each new computer generation came along, my husband, Fulton Wright, patiently moved my manuscript from one software package to the next, assuring me that I would readily learn the new languages and protocols. I affectionately acknowledge his guidance and his loving support.

N. K. W.
Prescott, Arizona
1992

Chapter Notes

Preface

1. Undated fragment, item 15, file folio 14, document box 2, Sharlot M. Hall Collection, Sharlot Hall Museum, Prescott, Arizona, hereinafter referred to as the SMH Collection.

***Biographical Introduction**—by Margaret F. Maxwell*

1. Sharlot Hall, "The Great Problem," unpublished essay, August 1914?, item 16, file folio 1, document box 3, SMH Collection.

2. Sharlot Hall to Arthur Upson, undated holograph letter, about 1898, item 12, file folio 2, document box 1, SMH Collection.

3. Sharlot Hall, unpublished, undated fragment, SMH Collection.

4. Ibid.

CHAPTER ONE
Child Life among the Moquis

1. Unpublished Navajo and Hopi notes, MS., item 5, file folio 2, document box 3, SMH Collection.

2. Byrd Granger, *Arizona's Names (X marks the Place),* (Tucson: Falconer Publishing Company, 1983) pp. 307, 420.

3. Margaret F. Maxwell, *A Passion for Freedom: the Life of Sharlot Hall,* (Tucson: The University of Arizona Press, 1982), p. 40.

4. Unpublished manuscript, item 2, file folio 9, document box 4, SMH Collection.

CHAPTER TWO
Log Book of a Mountain Schooner

1. Sharlot Hall, unpublished manuscript, "The Log Book of a Mountain Schooner: A Camping Trip through Northern Arizona," edited version of horseback trip from the Verde Valley to the Grand Canyon, July 11—August 11, 1893, file folio 7, document box 3, SMH Collection.

2. What are "mew flowers"? If any reader has a clue, please contact Sharlot Hall Museum. The editor would like to know.

3. Sharlot Hall, unpublished manuscript, "Log-Book of a Mountain Schooner," original version of horseback trip from the Verde Valley to the Grand Canyon, July 11—August 11, 1893, item 8, document box 5, SMH Collection.

CHAPTER THREE
Roadrunner

1. Sharlot Hall, *Poems of a Ranch Woman*, posthumously compiled by Josephine MacKenzie, with a biography by Charles Franklin Parker (Prescott, Arizona: Sharlot Hall Historical Society, 1953), p. 103.

2. Roger Tory Peterson, *Field Guide to Western Birds*, (Boston: Houghton Mifflin, 1941), p. 86.

3. Sharlot Hall, unpublished manuscript, item 6, file folio 3, document box 3, SMH Collection.

CHAPTER FOUR
The Trip to Roosevelt

1. Lawrence Clark Powell, *Arizona: A Bicentennial History*, (New York: W. W. Norton, 1976), pp. 76-77.

2. "Select Committee Will Name Points on Apache Trail," *Arizona Republican*, n.d., 1905. Clipping from the Davisson Collection, file folio 3, document box 131, Sharlot Hall Museum.

3. "The Massacre at Bloody Tanks" or "The Pinole Treaty" involved King Woolsey, a Prescott-area rancher, member of the first Territorial Legislative Assembly, a man with a wide reputation as an indefatigable Indian fighter. In May of 1864, Woolsey led a company of settlers against marauding Apaches in the Tonto Basin, south of the later Roosevelt Dam area. When he found he was encircled by Indians, he sent an Indian interpreter to offer gifts and invite the Apaches to a conference. After the Indians were seated Woolsey gave the signal to shoot them. Bad enough, but the appalling story goes on to say that the Indians were first sent a "gift" of pinole (ground, sweetened, toasted corn) laced with strychnine, causing about forty of them to die of poison. For the historical background of the affair, see Jay J. Wagoner, *Arizona Territory, 1863-1912: A Political History*, (Tucson: University of Arizona Press, 1980), pp. 21-22. And for the unsavory "pinole" account see Frank C. Lockwood, *The Apache Indians*, (Lincoln: University of Nebraska Press, 1938) pp. 148-150.

4. Sharlot M. Hall, notes penciled on both sides of eight pages of newsprint, item 5, file folder 1, document box 3, the SMH Collection. More material was later added to this manuscript, edited, and published as "The Great Tonto Storage Reservoir," *Out West*, November 1906, pp. 385-412.

CHAPTER FIVE
Alone: The Essential Sharlot

1. Sharlot Hall, *Cactus and Pine*, (Phoenix: Arizona Republican Print Shop, 1924), p. 169.

2. Margaret F. Maxwell, *A Passion for Freedom; the Life of Sharlot Hall*, (Tucson: University of Arizona Press, 1982), pp. 44-63.

3. Sharlot Hall, diary of Los Angeles trip, c. 1905, item 3, document box 8, the SMH Collection.

4. Sharlot Hall, letter to Alice Hewins, June 25, 1926, item 12, file folio 12, document box 1, SMH Collection.

CHAPTER SIX
Spring in the Desert

1. Maureen Ward, "Tree-ring Lab at Work on Phoenix Flood Control," *Arizona Wildcat*, Dec. 5, 1980, p. 1., quoted in Margaret F. Maxwell. See note 2.

2. Quoted with permission from Margaret F. Maxwell's unpublished manuscript, "Sharlot Hall's Desert."

3. Sharlot M. Hall, "When Spring Comes to the Desert," *Out West*, 22 (June 1905), pp. 263-378.

CHAPTER SEVEN
The Unmarried Woman

1. Sharlot Hall, "The Great Problem," unpublished essay, August 1914, item 16, file folio 1, document box 3, SMH Collection.

CHAPTER EIGHT
Lonesome Valley: Sharlot's Southwest

1. *Arizona State Business Directory*, Volume XXVI, (The Gazetteer Publishing and Printing Company, Denver, Colorado, 1938), p. 143.

2. Sharlot Hall, "Phrases, Hints, and Odds and Ends of Thought," 1897-1899, item 7, document box 5A, SMH Collection, p. 50.

3. Ibid., p. 96.

4. Ibid., p. 91.

5. Edward Sandford Martin, *The Unrest of Women*, (New York: Appleton, 1913).

6. Sharlot Hall, letter to Alice Hewins, January 19, 1914, item 14, file folio 7, document box 1, SMH Collection.

7. Sharlot Hall, letter to Alice Hewins, February 13, 1914, item 15, file folio 7, document box 1, SMH Collection.

8. Sharlot Hall, letter to Alice Hewins, May 11, 1914, item 19, file folio 7, document box 1, SMH Collection.

9. Sharlot Hall, letter to Tim Riordan, c. 1928, Northern Arizona Historical Society Collection, housed in the Special Collections Library, Northern Arizona University, Flagstaff, Arizona.

CHAPTER NINE
How Splendid Is Our Past

1. Sharlot Hall, "The House of a Thousand Hands," brochure printed by the Prescott Chamber of Commerce, 1935, item 8, file folio 1, document box 2, SMH Collection.

2. Governor George W. P. Hunt, letter to Sharlot Hall, February 23, 1928, item 4, file folio 13, document box 1, SMH Collection.

3. Sharlot Hall, letter to J. Andrew West, May 28, 1927, item 30, file folio 12, document box 1, SMH Collection.

4. Minutes, Common Council of the City of Prescott, June 6, 1927, vol. 9, pp. 230-31.

5. Sharlot Hall, typescript, item 1, file folio 8, document box 2, SMH Collection.

6. Sharlot Hall, letter to Timothy Riordan, undated, Northern Arizona Pioneers Society Collection, housed in the Special Collections Library, Northern Arizona University, Flagstaff, Arizona.

7. Sharlot Hall, letter to Timothy Riordan, August 21, 1928, Northern Arizona Pioneers Society Collection, housed in the Special Collections Library, Northern Arizona University, Flagstaff, Arizona.

8. Sharlot Hall, letter to Timothy Riordan, September 3, 1928, item 12a, file folio 13, document box 1, SMH Collection. "Texas Guinan" was the nickname given to motion picture actress and entertainer, Mary Louise Guinan, who was born in Waco, Texas, in 1884. She played western cowgirls armed with two revolvers, according to George E. Shankle, *American Nicknames: Their Origin and Significance.* 2d. ed. (New York: Wilson, 1955), p. 185.

9. Sharlot Hall, undated typescript of a talk on history, item 9, document box 8, SMH Collection.

CHAPTER TEN
Called to the Mat

1. Eric Partridge, *Dictionary of Slang and Unconventional English,* 6th ed., New York: MacMillan, 1967, p. 512.

2. Margaret F. Maxwell, *A Passion For Freedom: the Life of Sharlot Hall,* (Tucson: University of Arizona Press, 1982), pp. 191-192.

3. Sharlot Hall, diary, c. 1907, item 3, document box 8, SMH Collection.

4. Claudette Simpson gives a lucid account of this in "The Sharlot Hall Controversy," The *Prescott Courier* (Westward section) June 7, 1974.

5. "Some Facts by Miss Hall; Letter to Members of the Legislature Conveying Information Regarding the Proposed Office of State Historian," *Arizona Republican,* 31 May 1912.

6. Governor Hunt, letter to Sharlot Hall, June 3, 1912, Sharlot Hall Museum, Prescott, Arizona.

7. Sharlot Hall, letter to the Monday Club, March 1925, item 19, file folio 11, document box 1, SMH Collection.

8. This was Grace Chapman, Sharlot's longtime friend who was County Recorder of Yavapai County for many years. Sharlot had also supported Democrats Carl Hayden and Lewis W. Douglas. Maxwell, p. 192.

9. Sharlot Hall, "Call Miss Hall to G.O.P. 'Mat'," *Prescott Evening Courier,* October 24, 1932, pp. 1,7.

10. Sharlot Hall, quotes from old cowman, 1936, item 5, file folio 9, document box 2, SMH Collection.

CHAPTER ELEVEN
A Bit of Picturesque Western Profanity

1. Epitaph quoted in Sharlot Hall's grey book #1, 1905, item 6, document box 5, SMH Collection.

2. Erna Fergusson, *Our Southwest*, (New York: Knopf, 1940), p. 184.

3. Ibid., p. 185.

4. Sharlot Hall, "A Round of Dialect and Word Study," c. 1898, item 4, document box 7, SMH Collection.

5. Ibid.

6. Ibid.

7. Ibid.

8. Sharlot Hall, "The Old Hassayampers," notes on early miners, c. 1910, item 9, file folio 1, document box 3, SMH Collection.

CHAPTER TWELVE
Wind Song: Sharlot though the Eyes of Her Friends

1. Sharlot Hall, *Cactus and Pine*, (Phoenix, Arizona: Arizona Republican Print Shop, 1924), "Wind Song," verses 3-4, p. 146.

2. Sue Chamberlain Abbey, "Sharlot Hall," oral history tape no. 109. Sharlot Hall Museum, Prescott, Arizona.

3. Ibid.

4. Ida Williams Davisson, "My Memories of Sharlot," 1946, Davisson Collection, Arizona Historical Society, Tucson, Arizona.

5. A.M. MacDuffee, letter to Sharlot Hall, February 8, 1912, item 12, file folio 6, document box 1, SMH Collection.

6. Matthew Riordan, letter to Sharlot Hall, April 25, 1910, item 5, file folio 4, document box 1, SMH Collection.

7. Alice Hewins, "Sharlot Hall," Arizona State Archives, Phoenix, Arizona, p. 7.

8. Grace Sparkes, address to the Arizona Poetry Day observance, April 9, 1945, item 11, file folio 12, document box 3, SMH Collection.

9. Erna Fergusson, letter to Sharlot Hall, June 11, 1940, item 2, file folio 3, document box 4, SMH Collection.

10. Charles Franklin Parker, "The West of Long Ago," *Arizona Highways,* January 1943, p. 11.

Index

A
A-1 Cattle Company, 11, 18
Abbey, Sue Chamberlain, 87-88, 93
Agua Fria, 12
Alone, 41-45
"Alone," 42
Apache trail, 33
Apaches, 36, 96
Arizona, statehood of, xx
Arizona Federation of Women's Clubs, xx
Arizona Highways, 91
Arizona Lumber Company, 69
Arizona Pioneers Association, 85
Arizona Pioneers' Home, 85
Arizona Strip, xx
Arizona territorial historian, xx - xxi
Arizona territorial legislature, 74

B
Boblett, Adeline (Sharlot's mother). *See* Hall, Adeline Boblett
Boblett, Samuel Morgan (Sharlot's uncle), xv

C
Cactus and Pine, 97
Camp Verde, Arizona, 8
"Cash In," 92
Chino Valley, Arizona, 59
Coolidge, Calvin, 65, 75

D
Davis, Mr. and Mrs. John, 7-8, 12, 16, 22-23
Davisson, Ida, 88
Dawes, Charles, 75
Democratic Party, 79
Dewey, Arizona, 59, 62
Dixon, Maynard, xix

E
Edson, Charles Farwell, xix

F
Fergusson, Erna, 81-82, 91
Fish Creek Hill, 38-39
Flagstaff, 10-11
Fort Misery, xxi
Free Thought, 41-42

G
Gilman, Charlotte Perkins, xix
Goodwin, John, xxi
Governor's Mansion, xxi, 65-72
Graham, Margaret Collier, xix
Grand Canyon, 13, 17-25

H
Hall, Adeline Boblett (Sharlot's Mother), xvi, xxi, 56
Hall, James (Sharlot's father), xvi
Hall, Sharlot:
- childhood, xv
- death, xxii
- editor, *Land of Sunshine* and *Out West*, xix
- education, xvii, 88
- on herself, 41-45
- opinions about conservation, 10-11
- opinions about friendship, 43-45
- opinions about love and marriage, xvi, 41-42
- opinions of men, xvi, 55-58, 84
- philosophy of, 55-58

poetry of, xiv, 25-27, 87, 92
political views, 73-80
presidential elector, 75
speeches, 85-86
ranch life, xvii
territorial historian, xx-xxi
"When Spring Comes to the Desert," 47-54

"Hassayampers," 85-86
Hewins, Alice, xxi, 43, 61-63, 90
Hopi Indians, 1-6
Howard, Judge, xxi
Hunt, George W. P., xxi, 74

J

James, George Wharton, xix

L

Land of Sunshine, xix. *See also* *Out West*
Loneliness, 41-45
Lonesome Valley, 59-63
Lummis, Charles F., xix, 43
Lynx Creek, xvi, xxi

M

MacDuffee, A. M., 89
Markham, Edwin, xix
Marriage, Free Thought, views on, xvi, 41-42
Maxwell, Margaret F., xi-xii, xv-xxii, 41, 47, 73, 93
Men, Sharlot Hall's views on, xvi
Mescal bake, 54
Miller, Joaquin, xix
Monday Club, 75
Moody, Charles Amadon, xix
Moquis, 1-6. *See also* Hopi Indians 32

N

Navajo Indians, 29-30

O

O'Neill, Buckey, 72
Orchard Ranch, xvi, xxi, 59
Out West, xix, 43, 47. *See also* *Land of Sunshine*

P

Parker, Charles Franklin, 91
Pinole Treaty, 36, 96
Poems of a Ranch Woman, 96
Powell, Lawrence Clark, xi, 96
Prescott, Arizona, xvi-xvii, xxi, 66
Putnam, Samuel P., xix, 41-42

R

Republican Party, 73-80
Riordan, Denis Matthew, xix, 61, 89
Riordan, Timothy, 69-71, 99
Roadrunner, 27-32
"Roadrunner," poem, 27
Roosevelt, Arizona, 33
Roosevelt, Theodore, 33
Roosevelt Dam, 33-40

S

Salt River, 33, 36
Seiber, Al, 36
Sharlot Hall Museum, xii, xxi-xxii, 81
Simpson, Claudette, 99
Sloan, Richard E., xx, 74
Sparkes, Grace, 91

T

Territorial historian. *See* Arizona territorial historian
Tonto Creek, 39

U

Unmarried woman, the, 55-58
Upson, Arther. *See* Biographical Introduction, Note 2, 95
U.S. Bureau of Reclamation, 33

W

Wail of the Weary Eight," 25-26
Walpi, 2
West, J. Andrew, Prescott city attorney, 66
Westover, Myron, 89
"When Spring Comes to the Desert," 47-54
Wide Awake, 1
"Wind Song," 87
Winsor, Mulford, xxi, 74
"With a Box of Apples," xiv
Women, Sharlot Hall's views on, xvi, 55-58
Woolsey, King, 36, 96

Y

Yavapai College, xi-xii, 93
Yavapai County, 66, 68, 79

Printed and Designed by Graphic Impressions, Inc.
Prescott, Arizona

Bound by Central Bindery, Phoenix,
Arizona
Printed on 80# Warren Lustro Dull white acid-free text
with 100# Lustro Dull Cream
Typeset by Graphic Impressions, Inc.
with Lucida Bright 11 over 12 and Monotype
Cursive Bold Italic